Start playing the Queen's Gambit

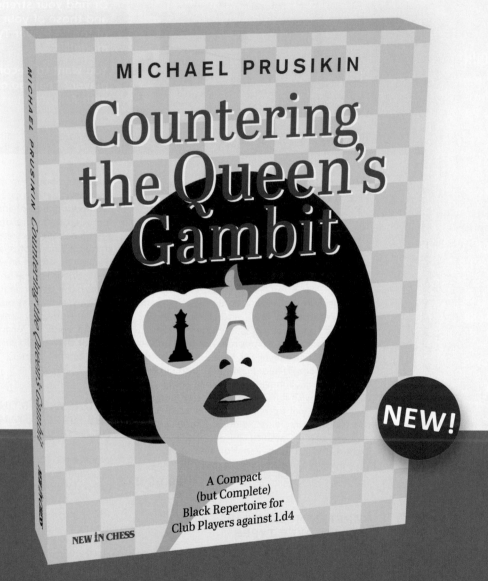

2022#2

NEW IN CHESS

Contents

'Chess players tend to see everything in black and white.'

CONTRIBUTORS TO THIS ISSUE
James Altucher, Jonas Bjerre, Magnus Carlsen, Arjun Erigaisi, Jorden van Foreest, Anish Giri, John Henderson, Shakhriyar Mamedyarov, Dylan McClain, Peter Heine Nielsen, Maxim Notkin, Judit Polgar, Matthew Sadler, Han Schut, Gregory Serper, Jan Timman, Thomas Willemze

The Battle of the Sexes

n the last day of 2021, Gibraltar's iconic Caleta Hotel, built into the cliffs overlooking Catalan Bay, sadly closed its doors after almost 60 years. The building is now in the process of being demolished to make way for a new five-star Hilton. Yet, despite Covid restrictions and the loss of a much-loved tournament venue, the top chess tradition on the Rock nevertheless continued.

Filling the gap this year for the traditional Gibraltar Masters was the novel one-off event of 'The Battle of the Sexes Tournament'. Held at the venerable Garrison Library, founded in 1793, 'the Battle' was a £100,000 match between ten female professionals and ten male players, equally matched by rating and age. Not surprisingly, both teams included several Gibraltar Masters regulars, such as GMs Sabino Brunello, Joe Gallagher, Pia Cramling and Antoaneta Stefanova . The two teams were quickly dubbed 'Team Pia' and 'Team Sabino' after their respective captains. And despite the women's team getting off to a promising flying start, the highly competitive match eventually ended in a 53-47 victory for the men's side. ∎

JOHN SAUNDERS

The Wall Street Shuffle

I t's not often we find ourselves trawling through reports in the *Financial Times* or *The Wall Street Journal*, but these days with the growth of the online game that's where you can find some of the hottest chess news. And this one involves the biggest name in the game partnering with one of the world's leading science and technology investors.

Play Magnus Group announced in January that the Russian-Israeli billionaire Yuri Milner and his wife Julia, through their Breakthrough Initiatives Limited company, had

Magnus Carlsen and Yuri Milner: sometimes great minds do think alike.

offered to buy $10 million worth of shares in the Norwegian company. An extraordinary shareholder meeting was called to decide on the private placement of the philanthropic couple, which went through without a hitch.

The link-up, coupled with strong growth of Play Magnus Group, will allow the company to improve and grow, and further shape the Champions Chess Tour into the leading chess circuit with global partners and audiences. 'Like science and mathematics, chess is one of the most advanced and creative pursuits of the human mind', said Yuri Milner on the deal. 'This investment will support Magnus and his team, and help foster the growth of chess worldwide – especially online.'

Magnus Carlsen and the Milners have been friends for years, and the World Champion added: 'This investment will help bring the sport to a larger audience. The chess world and the tech industry are closely interlinked, and for us to now have some of the greatest minds in the tech industry officially involved is encouraging.'

Show Me the Money

A lso making it into the financial papers in January was another online chess platform going for growth, with the news that General Atlantic, a leading global growth equity investor with $86 billion in assets, has now become a significant investor in California-headquartered Chess.com.

'Our mission is simple: help people enjoy chess', said Chess.com CEO and co-founder Erik Allebest. 'As a mission-driven, bootstrapped company that never raised venture funding, we knew we needed an experienced, savvy partner to help us in our next stage of growth. General Atlantic has a longstanding commitment to partnership in helping companies grow and thrive, and we are beyond excited to work with them to bring the joy of chess to millions more across the globe.'

'As interest in chess continues to grow, we believe Chess.com has an opportunity to make this classic

Chess.com CEO Erik Allebest wants to bring chess to millions more across the globe.

game even more accessible to new and existing players around the world', added Anton Levy, a co-president and managing director at General Atlantic on the partnership. 'We are thrilled to support Chess.com's vision to leverage technology to further build the global chess community and look forward to partnering with Erik and the team to grow the platform.'

Going for Gold

C hess is fast becoming a million dollar game, literally! Windsor Jewelers, one of the US's premier independent jewellery stores based in Augusta, Georgia, recently gushed in a press release that they have one of the most expensive chess sets in the world up for sale.

The set was one of the most popular

White gold begins, but they say yellow gold is OK.

attractions at the Gemological Institute of America Museum in California when it was shown there last year. The pieces are made of 14 karat yellow and white gold and adorned with gemstones. There is nearly 11 pounds of gold in the set and it took four artists nearly one year to carve the wax models used to cast the pieces.

It was originally commissioned and completed in 1971 for an avid chess-playing prominent doctor from Massachusetts and has been in the private collection of only two families since. Oh, the price we hear you ask? A mere snip they say at just $1 million!

Rocket Man

With the ability to land more quads than anyone else, US men's figure skater Nathan Chen exorcised his demons from 2018 to finally win gold at the recent Winter Olympics in Beijing. The Olympian's secret weapon? Well, it turns out it was chess!

Nathan 'Chess' Chen with his Olympic gold medal.

In an interview for *GQ* magazine following his success in Beijing, Chen – dubbed 'Rocket Man' for his aerial abilities – revealed he came from a 'huge chess family'. As a kid he frequented chess tournaments and he says the game helped him focus better on his skills.

Chess became a metaphor for the 22-year-old skater, and instead of getting emotional, he tries to solve any problem in life and on the ice as he would solve a puzzle on a chessboard. 'With chess, it's always go for the king', he told *GQ*. 'So if you're able, have that mindset. What are you trying to go for? Go full force at it. Know that there are other forces at play, but never really give up, and keep attacking for the goals that you want.'

Super Bowl Chess

The halftime show and the ads at the Super Bowl are often the highlight of the annual glitzy American Football extravaganza. This year

it was promoted by Pepsi with the video 'The Call' that featured chess, probably seen more than 100 million times. Among the artists in the ad at the board – and also performing live at halftime – were rappers and chess aficionados Dr Dre and Kendrick Lamar.

At the same time, this year's Super Bowl LVI between the Cincinnati Bengals and Los Angeles Rams wasn't only referred to by the great football cliché of being a 'chess match' by coaches, players and broadcasters, it also took the game right into the locker-room with media features on the chess prowess of Cincinnati quarterback Joe Burrow.

The Bengals talisman has been a competitive chess player since he began playing in elementary school in Ohio. He rekindled his interest in the game through the Netflix series

Bengals quarterback Joe Burrow likes to keep his pawns close to his chest.

The Queen's Gambit, becoming such a big fan that he purchased a signed first edition copy of Walter Tevis's acclaimed novel. During a 2021 press conference, Burrow said: 'Chess is fun. It's very strategic, and you have to plan all your moves.'

He attributed the Bengals successful run to the Super Bowl this year by playing his gridiron teammates at speed chess before games. Burrows even played online on Chess.com to relax before the big event. His chess skills almost paid off as the Bengals narrowly lost 20-23 to the Rams.

Children of the Knight

It sounds a little like *Buffy: The Vampire Slayer* meets Beth Harmon of *The Queen's Gambit* fame meets *Twilight*'s Bella Swan, but that's the premise of author J.S. Furlong's *Hidden City*, the first book in her 'The Unimaginables' series.

According to the blurb of the vampiric fantasy, it all revolves around nerdy New York City high-schooler Stacy Goldman who has everything she could want: a loving family, supportive friends and academic prowess. She also just happens to be a chess whiz and doesn't believe in anything she can't prove. Especially monsters and things that go bump in the night.

But after enrolling in the challenging St Ignatius' College Preparatory Academy in Richmond, Virginia, she falls in with two other outsiders, Finder and Tully to reveal a big secret after they witness a brutal and bloodthirsty attack.

With her chess-playing abilities proving crucial to the plot, will newfound vampire hunter Stacy be able to discover her own untapped belief in

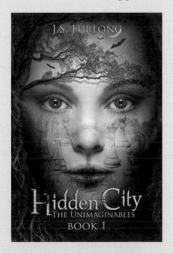

Luckily Stacy Goldman is also a chess whiz…

the unimaginable to save not only the life of one of the supernatural fiends she's befriended but also those of herself and her friends? ∎

Here comes Hikaru

Free of pressure Nakamura uses wildcard to win Berlin Grand Prix

Following a break of 822(!) days, streaming king Hikaru Nakamura returned to the board to try his hand at classical chess again. In Berlin the American ace confidently won the first of three GP's (true, in the rapid tiebreak of the final) and holds an excellent position to qualify for the Candidates tournament. **JOHN HENDERSON** reports.

The road to World Champion Magnus Carlsen directly runs through Berlin this year. The German capital provides the bookends to three FIDE Grand Prix tournaments being staged through February-April: two in Berlin and one in the Serbian capital of Belgrade. The top finishers will earn the last two spots into the Candidates Tournament in Madrid, Spain, this summer.

Already six players (of eight) have qualified so far for the Candidates: Alireza Firouzja (France) and Fabiano Caruana (USA) from the FIDE Grand Swiss; Jan-Krzysztof Duda (Poland) and Sergey Karjakin (Russia) from the FIDE World Cup; Ian Nepomniachtchi (Russia) as loser of the 2021 World Championship Match; plus FIDE wildcard nominee Teimour Radjabov (Azerbaijan).

Billed by the World Chess organizers as 'Time to say Berlin', the opening leg of the FIDE Grand Prix

Hikaru Nakamura stands centre stage in the early rounds of his first over-the-board tournament in more than two years. The American would remain centre stage till the very last day.

got off to an inauspicious Covid start with the late news that China's world number 3, Ding Liren, had to withdraw due to a series of visa mishaps coupled with stricter pandemic guidelines at home that came into force in the run-up to the Beijing Winter Olympics.

Several of the top Chinese players missed out in big events recently due to the ongoing lockdown/visa restrictions, with notable absences in the Tata Steel Masters, the World Rapid & Blitz Championships, plus the World Cup. It was later confirmed that Ding would also have to miss the Belgrade Grand Prix, so he's effectively out of the Candidates without even getting a chance to make a move. It's sad to see a force as Ding not getting a potential title shot through no fault of his own, but there was nothing FIDE could do under the circumstances.

In the end China's loss proved to be the US's gain, as it only strengthened their hand in the opening Grand Prix. Leading the charge in Berlin was Wesley So, Levon Aronian (playing officially for the first time under the colours of the Stars and Stripes), Leinier Dominguez, and last but not least Hikaru Nakamura. 'Naka' had last played a classical game back in October 2019 at the FIDE Grand Swiss, and being otherwise pre-occupied streaming to more than a million chess followers on his popular Twitch channel, he needed a wildcard spot from FIDE president Arkady Dvorkovich – much to the chagrin of his Russian compatriots – to compete.

Indeed, it was the US quartet – none of whom born in the country, but then again they are a nation largely built on immigrants – who all dominated the early double round-robin stages in Berlin that were to determine who would go through to the 'business end' of the four-player knockout as pool winners. Wesley So made all the early running in Pool D and looked a virtual shoo-in for a qualifying spot after he beat Dominguez.

Leinier Dominguez
Wesley So
Berlin FIDE Grand Prix 2022
Pool D (4)

position after 24...♘d3

25.♗c2
Dominguez has managed to weather the storm to reach this position – but it only takes a few very accurate

'Naka' had last played a classical game back in October 2019 at the FIDE Grand Swiss

moves from So to turn the game into a winning double-rook ending.
25...♖f2!

26.♗xd3? In hindsight, a better way to hold was 26.♖e3! ♖xd2 27.♖xd3 ♖xd3 28.♗xd3.
26...♖xd2 27.♗xg6 hxg6 28.♖e7 ♖xb2 29.♖ce1

29...♖f8!
So's rooks get to the seventh first.
30.♖d7 ♖ff2 31.♖ee7 ♖xg2+ 32.♔f1 ♔h7 33.h4
Attempting to worry Black with the threat of a mating net – but So is ahead of the game. The problem is that the straightforward 33.♖xg7+ ♔h6 34.♖h7+ ♔g5 35.♖xb7 ♖bf2+ 36.♔e1 ♖xa2 37.♔f1 ♖xg3 is easily winning for Black.
33...♔h6!

34.♖e5 If 34.♖xg7 ♖bf2+ 35.♔e1 ♔h5! 36.♖xb7 ♖xa2 is much the same as the above note.
34...♖bf2+ 35.♔e1 ♖xa2 36.♔f1 ♖h2 37.♔g1 ♖ag2+ 38.♔f1 ♖b2

Threatening mate and defending b7.
39.♔g1 ♖hd2 White resigned.

Soon, however, So regretted not making the most of his early lead. In a dramatic reversal of fortunes, Dominguez staged a late rally to force a speed tiebreak-decider, which the former Cuban duly won. A dejected So was left to reflect in his post-defeat interview just how cruel chess can be at times: 'I have to go home, which is not ideal, but that's what chess is: you train so hard and then everything really depends on that crucial few seconds of decision-making that determines what will happen in your tournament.'

'I'm a new American'
Meanwhile in Pool C, newly-minted American Levon Aronian, now resident in the chess Mecca of Saint Louis, rolled back the years to easily gain his knockout spot with a vintage performance. Aronian was determined to prove his worth to his new

Wesley So looked to be on course for the knockout stage, but then 'that crucial few seconds of decision-making that determines what will happen' sent the American home.

compatriots: 'I'm a new American,' he proudly proclaimed in victory. 'I have to prove I can be as good as them, or even better.'

The former Armenia number 1 not only breezed through, he did so with a series of steadfast and confident performances. With his win against 17-year-old German prodigy Vincent Keymer the veteran jumped up the world rankings to topple Fabiano Caruana from his top dog perch. On the March FIDE Rating List Aronian will be the new US number 1 and world number 4.

Next to qualify for the knockout stage was Hikaru Nakamura, as he too found a new lease of life with his wildcard entry. Despite his hiatus of over two years – 822(!) days for those

Newly-minted American Levon Aronian: 'I have to prove I can be as good as them, or even better'

officially counting – without playing a classical game, the five-time US champion all but sailed through as the confident winner of Pool A. En route he outwitted his two main Russian rivals, Alexander Grischuk and Andrey Esipenko, who were seen as favourites to qualify from what was widely perceived to be the 'Group of Death'.

Hikaru Nakamura
Alexander Grischuk
Berlin FIDE Grand Prix 2022
Pool A (5)

position after 29...♖f7

30.♗c1! A strategic retreat.
30...♕d8 31.♗b2
The pressure down the long a1-h8 diagonal is reaching critical mass.
31...♕f8 32.♔g2!

Just a couple more accurate moves from Nakamura, and Grischuk is left for dead.
32...♗d8 33.♕f3 ♗c8 34.♕e3!
♖xb3 35.axb3 fxg5
Grischuk might have held out a little longer with 35...♗e7, but after 36.b4! ultimately Black is doomed.
36.♕c3 ♖xf1

37.♕h8+! ♔f7 38.♕xh7+ ♔e8
39.♕xg6+ Not falling for the trap of 39.♗xf1 ♗h3+!!.
39...♔e7 40.♕xg5+ ♖f6 Grischuk could have held out longer with 40...♔d7, but after 41.♕g7+! ♖f7 42.♕xf8 ♖xf8 43.h7 the double-bishop ending a pawn up will be easily won for White.
41.h7 ♔d7 42.♕g8!

The pawn can't be stopped now. Black resigned.

Smooth and impressive

With a trio of US players already into the knockout stage, standing in the way of a possible American victory in Berlin stood the lone figure of Richard Rapport. The enterprising young Hungarian managed to beat Poland's Radoslaw Wojtaszek in a close tiebreak-decider to win Pool B.

Rapport's reward was a semi-final match-up with the very-much in-form Nakamura, with Aronian and Dominguez left to battle it out in the other semifinal. By this stage there was just no stopping a rampant Nakamura, who with a smooth and impressive opening game win over Rapport all but ripped the Hungarian's spirit. Nakamura's win was enough for a 1½-½ defeat and a place in the final.

NOTES BY
Jan Timman

Hikaru Nakamura
Richard Rapport
Berlin FIDE Grand Prix 2022
Semi-Final Game 1
Queen's Gambit Declined, Exchange Variation

1.d4 ♘f6 2.c4 e6 3.♘c3 d5
4.cxd5 exd5 5.♗g5 c6 6.♕c2
♗e7 7.e3 ♘bd7 8.♗d3 ♘h5

A solid system. The bishop swap allows Black to mobilize more quickly.
9.♗xe7 ♕xe7 10.0-0-0 ♘b6 11.h3
g6 12.♘f3 ♘g7 13.g4 ♗e6
Ulf Andersson always played his bishop to d7 in this position, antici-
pating White's standard plan in this line: the manoeuvre ♘c3-a4 after both players have castled kingside.
14.♘e2

We see Nakamura following a different plan: he is going to take his knight to f4 to increase White's influence in the centre.
14...0-0-0 15.♔b1 ♔b8 16.♖c1

16...♘e8 The alternative was 16...h5 17.g5 ♗f5, but then White has a slight plus after 18.♘f4 ♘c4 19.♗xf5 ♘xf5 20.h4. The text is intended to direct the knight to vital squares via d6.
17.♘f4 ♘d6 18.a4 Instead of his knight, White plays his pawn to a4. The position is getting sharp: how is Black going to react to this putative attack?

Hikaru Nakamura leans back, knowing that the job is done.
There is no way for Richard Rapport to save the ending.

18...♘dc4

Rapport picks up the gauntlet. The alternative was 18...♗c8, after which White will find it hard to make progress on the queenside, since Black is solid after 19.a5 ♘bc4 20.a6 b5!. White's best bet is the cautious 19.b3, but it won't yield him an advantage.

19.a5!

The deep point of the previous move.

19...♕b4!

The best reaction. If Black bites with 19...♘xa5, White forces a favourable endgame with 20.♕c5. After 20...♕xc5 21.dxc5 ♘d7 22.b4 ♘c4 23.♗xc4 dxc4 he won't need to recap-

ture the pawn at once. Far stronger is 24.♘g5!, with a large advantage for White.

20.♕c3 Preventing the knight mate
on a3 and forcing a queen swap.

20...♕xa5 21.♕xa5 ♘xa5
22.♘g5 It's clear that White has ample compensation and can recapture the pawn if he wants. Black's first priority now is covering the f-pawn.

22...♖df8

23.♗xg6

A spectacular move, but a good alternative was 23.♘fxe6 fxe6 24.f4. The idea of this pawn sacrifice is that it yields White a strong kingside initiative. After 24...♘ac4 25.♖ce1 ♖f6

26.♘f3 White is ready to advance his h-pawn. Black will find it harder to get his queenside majority moving.

23...♘b3

Black is looking for further complications. Simply 23...hxg6 would probably have been stronger. After 24.♘gxe6, 24...♖fg8 is the most accurate rook move. There could follow: 25.♘c5 g5 26.♘h5 ♘ac4, and all four knights are well-positioned. The position is equal.

24.♘fxe6

White had two alternatives:
– 24.♘xh7 ♖c8 25.♗d3 ♘xc1 26.♖xc1 ♗d7 27.♘h5, and White has the initiative;
– 24.♖c3 hxg6 25.♘gxe6 fxe6 26.♖xb3 ♖hg8 27.♖c3 ♘c4 28.♗d3, with some advantage for White.

24...fxe6 25.♘xh7

25...♖fg8

25...♖xf2 would probably have been stronger. It was hard to see over the board that Black would have sufficient counterplay after 26.♖c2 ♘d2+ 27.♔a2 ♘bc4 28.♖d1 ♖f3 29.♖cxd2 ♘xd2 30.♖xd2 ♖xh3 31.♘f6. The white passed pawn seems strong, but Black just manages to hold, as witness: 31...♖8h6 32.♘d7+ ♔c7 33.♘e5 ♖xe3 34.g5 ♖hh3 35.♗f2 ♖hg3 36.♖f7+ ♔b6 37.♘d7+ ♔b5, and the black king is safe enough.

26.♗d3

The computer has a slight preference for 26.♗c2, which has a deep point. In the line 26...♘xc1 27.♔xc1 ♖g7 28.♘f6 ♖h6 29.♘h5 ♖g8 White now has 30.♔d1!, after which he can meet 30...♘c4 with 31.b3 ♘d6 32.♔e2, with advantage.

26...♘xc1 27.♔xc1 ♖g7 28.♘f6

28...♖f7

A serious error. With 28...♖h6 Black could have prevented further expansion on the kingside. The position is equal, e.g. 29.♘h5 ♖g8 30.♔d1 ♘c4 31.b3, and now the difference between 26.♗d3 and 26.♗c2 becomes clear: Black swaps the strong white bishop with 31...♘b2+.

29.g5

Of course. Now Black is forced to sacrifice an exchange; the mighty white knight must be eliminated.

29...♖xf6 30.gxf6 ♖f8 31.h4 ♖xf6 32.h5

Materially speaking, the position is equal again, but the h-pawn is very strong. Black is facing an uphill struggle, but he'll probably just be able to hold.

32...♖h6 33.♗d2 ♔c7 34.♔e2

34...♔d6

Hurrying the king to the wing that's under attack is obvious enough, but 34...♘c4, adding the knight to the defence first, would have been stronger. There could follow: 35.b3 ♘d6 36.♔f3 ♔d7 37.♔g4 ♔e7,

ANALYSIS DIAGRAM

and now the point of Black's defence is revealed: he can prevent the white king and rook from penetrating. White's best bet is to continue with 38.f3 ♘f7 39.♗g6, after which Black will have his hands full defending.

35.♔f3 ♔e7 36.♔g4

Celeb 64

John Henderson

Jason Statham

Right at the start of his screen career, high-octane Hollywood hardman Jason Statham made his debut in the films of Guy Ritchie. Their first collaboration, *Lock, Stock and Two Smoking Barrels* (1998), started a friendship that was bonded over the chessboard.

Ritchie loves to play chess during downtimes on his movies, but the action flick director was surprised to discover – despite having a chess coach – that he was no match for the emerging English actor. And over what became a fierce chess rivalry, Ritchie hatched a remarkable plot for a chess-themed movie that was to become Statham's first leading role. In Ritchie's thriller *Revolver* (2005), Statham plays a scheming gambler. While in prison for a crime he didn't commit, Green discovers a formulaic game-winning strategy with the help of two inmates, two chess masters who also happen to be master fraudsters. From them he picks up invaluable 64-square strategic tips to masterplan his revenge on his release.

Ritchie and Statham recently reunited, in the new heist/crime thriller *Wrath Of Man* (2021). And even before the first day of shooting, their chess rivalry was also renewed, with Statham posting across his social media platforms a photo of his chess set with a message to remind Ritchie to bring his wallet! Statham's chess set also had a cameo in the movie, appearing as a prop in his 'H' character's Los Angeles lair. ∎

Black's problems are becoming clear: he must control square g5; but then the white rook will penetrate.

36...♔f6 37.♖h3 ♘c8 38.♖f3+ ♔g7 39.♔g6 ♘d6 40.♔g5 a5 41.♖f4

41...♘e4+

Desperation. But 41...a4 42.f3 would have made no difference either – White's e-pawn is going to e5.

42.♗xe4 dxe4 43.♖xe4 ♖f6 44.f4 This rook ending will not cause White any technical problems.

44...♖f5+ 45.♔g4 ♖b5 46.♖xe6 a4 47.♖e7+ ♔h6 48.♖e8 ♖xb2 49.♖h8+ ♔g7 50.♖a8 b5 51.e4 ♖a2 52.♖a7+ ♔h6 53.♖a6 ♔h7 54.♖a7+ ♔h6 55.♖a6 ♔h7 56.e5 b4 57.e6 b3 58.♔f5 ♖a1 59.♖b6 ♖e1 60.♔f6

60...♖e4

60...a3 would have been no good either, since White would sacrifice his rook: 61.♖xb3 a2 62.♖a3 a1♕ 63.♖xa1 ♖xa1 64.e7 ♖e1 65.♔f7, and wins.

61.e7 ♖xf4+ 62.♔e5 ♖f1 63.♔d6 ♖e1 64.♔d7 c5 65.dxc5 ♖d1+ 66.♔c7 ♖e1 67.♔d6 ♖d1+ 68.♔c6 ♖e1 69.♖b4 b2 70.♖xb2

♖xe7 71.♖a2

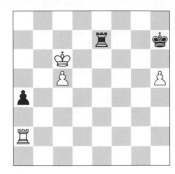

Black resigned.

■ ■ ■

Quizzed on the official FIDE/World Chess live stream about reaching the final, Nakamura was candid in victory: 'It's nice I guess. Probably not expected, but I felt that I have played well. I don't think I have done anything super-special, but when you are solid, and you take advantage of the few opportunities you have, then good things seem to happen.' And indeed more good things were about to happen.

Meanwhile, Aronian turned in an equally impressive 1½-½ victory over Dominguez, which led to an all-American final. And a surprising

Nakamura: 'When you are solid, and you take advantage of the few opportunities you have, then good things seem to happen'

one at that, as it defied all the pre-tournament odds by being contested by two veterans on the Candidates comeback trail!

Aronian's win against Dominguez was a gripping fight that was wonderful to watch.

NOTES BY
Jorden van Foreest

Levon Aronian
Leinier Dominguez
Berlin FIDE Grand Prix 2022
Semi-Final Game 1
Queen's Gambit Accepted, Greco Variation

1.d4 d5 2.c4 dxc4 No surprises here, as Leinier Dominguez has been playing the QGA almost exclusively for a while already.
3.e4 b5 4.a4 c6 5.axb5 cxb5 6.♘c3

6...♕b6 Not until long ago Black players had only been trying 6... a6, which, although interesting, is deemed somewhat dubious. Only very recently the text appeared on the scene and by now numerous high-level games have been played here. In fact, Dominguez had played this exact way earlier in the tournament against Wesley So.
7.♘d5 The aforementioned game featured 7. b3. Aronian however has whole different plans, as he goes for the most aggressive and direct attempt.
7...♕b7

8.♗f4 With ♘c7+ being threatened, Black has to whip up counterplay really fast.
8...e5!

Liberating the bishop on f8 with tempo is crucial.
9.♗xe5 ♘d7!

10.♗f4
One step back to go two steps forward. One shouldn't fall for the temptation of already going for the rook: 10.♘c7+ ♚d8 11.♘xa8 ♗b4+ 12.♚e2. The Bongcloud is not always good. It's almost never good: 12...♕xe4 mate.
10...♘gf6
Finally, Black has no longer a way to salvage his rook, but in return he gained a huge lead in development.

Calm after the storm. Levon Aronian won and Leinier Dominguez lost, but they both remain fascinated by the sharp fight they have just concluded.

11.♘c7+! Only now!
11...♚d8 12.♘xa8 ♕xe4+
12...♗b4+ 13.♗d2 is the major difference compared to the line starting with 10.♘c7+.
13.♘e2 ♕xa8

Despite having lost the exchange and the right to castle, Black has good compensation, as his pieces will all develop very smoothly to great squares and the white king is by no means safe either. One could argue that the most surprising thing about this crazy position is that up to this moment both players had been blitzing all of their moves!
14.f3

A multi-purpose move: it obstructs the a8-h1 diagonal and it creates some air for the king on f2.
From this moment onwards Dominguez started using lots of time, while Aronian was evidently still in his preparation.
14...♘d5 15.♗g5+!

A crafty move, forcing Black to make an uncomfortable decision.
15...f6
15...♘7f6 was certainly possible as well, but that would have been met all the same with 16.♗d2, when ♗a5+ is suddenly a lot harder to deal with, as there is no ...♘7b6 option anymore.
16.♗d2 ♗d6 17.♘g3?!

Perhaps this is a small inaccuracy by Aronian, as it immediately gives Black a target of attack. It would have been more clever to start with 17.♔f2, keeping both ♘g3 and ♘c3 as viable ideas.

18.♗e2! was called for, since despite gaining a pawn Black has to part with his strong dark-squared bishop after the trades: 18...♗xg3+ 19.hxg3 ♕xg3+ 20.♔f1.

Now 20.♖e1 ♗xd4+ is a disaster, so White has to offer an unfavourable trade with 20.♗a5 ♕f4!, giving Black a fantastic position.
19.♗e2 ♗c7 Now this idea works not as well. **20.♖e1**

17...♕b8! 18.♔f2?
Logical, as it defends the knight and prepares the slow development of his pieces on the kingside, but this is a serious mistake giving Black all of a sudden chance of seizing the initiative.

18...♖e8? Letting White off the hook. As the following moves show Dominguez did have the right idea but only executed it one move too late, changing the whole nature of the game. The immediate 18...♗c7! was called for, as now White is not in time to hide his king as in the game: 19.♗e2 ♗b6

20...♗b6?! According to the computers, 20...a6 would still have kept the balance, but it strikes me as an extremely hard move to contemplate, especially considering that Black has just gone ...♗c7, clearly intending the text-move.

21.♔g1! This is the difference and must have been a huge blow for Dominguez: the white king is just in time to tuck itself away in the corner. Capturing on d4 now would be disastrous for Black, as he only opens lines of fire towards his own king.

21...♘e5?
This rerouting of the knight is just too slow and not meeting the demands of the position. Somewhat strangely the way to keep the position together was by using the same square, however with the queen!
21...♕e5! is a quirky way to suddenly bring the queen back into the game and definitely not at all an easy one to spot. Still, according to the silicon monsters Black is alive and kicking here.
22.♔h1 ♘c6 23.b3! An excellent move by Aronian. Breaking up the pawn structure makes the whole black position fall apart.
23...c3 24.♗xb5!

24...♗d7 24...♖xe1+ is fairly similar to the game, and doesn't offer much hope either: 25.♗xe1 ♘xd4 26.♗c4 ♕e5 and for a moment Black seems to have restored some coordination,

and had his king been on b8 instead, he might even have enough compensation. As it is, Black is completely pinned on the d-file and is bound to lose more material quickly after, for example, 27.♖c1.
25.♖xe8+ ♗xe8

It's somewhat mysterious that the game even lasted 15 more moves from here, to be honest. Not only is White completely winning, he was also up more than an hour on the clock.
26.♗e1 26.♗xc6 might have been the cleanest way to win, although it does require a bit of calculation: 26...♗xc6 27.♗xc3! ♘xc3 28.♕c2 ♗xd4 29.♕d3 ♕e5 30.♘f5 ♘b5 31.♖d1 and finally Black can no longer hold on to his bishop.

26...♘xd4 27.♗xe8 c2
Trying to confuse matters...
28.♕d3 ♔xe8
With the passed pawn on c2 there are still a couple of tricks in the position. However, with some prudent moves, all Black's counterplay and trickery can be resolved.

29.♗d2? Suddenly Aronian makes a huge error!
29.♘e2!, offering the trade, would have saved White from some further headaches. Black has no way to keep the foot soldier on c2 much longer. A sample line goes as follows: 29...♕e5 30.♘xd4 ♗xd4 31.♖c1 ♘e3 32.♗g3! ♕c5 33.♗f4 ♘d1 34.♕e2+ ♔f7 35.♖xc2 ♘f2+ 36.♔g1 ♘h3+ 37.♔f1

SHALL I KEEP THE LITTLE LIGHT ON SIR?... AND I CHECKED THREE TIMES: THERE IS NO OPPONENT UNDER YOUR BED

BEREND VONK

♘xf4 38.♖xc5 ♘xe2 39.♖c7+ ♔g6 40.♔xe2 and White wins.

29...♕e5!

Forcing the white rook to move, as

...♘xf3 and ...♘xb3 are among the threats.

30.♖c1 f5! Highly resourceful play, keeping the white knight at bay for the time being.

31.♘c4 ♘e3? Very short of time, Dominguez makes a decisive error. The right idea, but it was necessary to prepare this jump first: 31...f4! 32.♘e4 ♘e3!. Having the knight protected by the pawn is crucial, despite allowing the white knight back into the game. Now the white queen checks don't lead anywhere, and the c2-pawn gives sufficient counterplay.

32.♕c8+ ♔f7 33.♕d7+ ♔g6 34.f4!

In comparison to 31...f4, the black queen is no longer capable of keeping its strong central position.

34...♕e6 34...♕xf4 35.♕e8+ was the point. **35.♕xe6+ ♘xe6 36.♘e2! ♘g4 37.g3 ♘c5 38.b4 ♘d3 39.♖xc2** Finally White is able to round up the menacing c2-pawn. **39...♘gf2+ 40.♔g2 ♘e4 41.♘c1!**

There is no point in continuing the endgame a full exchange down, and therefore Dominguez resigned. A great fighting game.

Nakamura's speed skills

The final proved to be a more tense affair with both games ending in relatively solid and workman-like draws. Then it unexpectedly swung wildly to the wildcard when it came to the rapid tiebreak-decider. Nakamura's speed skills emphatically came to the fore, but not before what should have been an easily drawing ♖+♙ ending went a little haywire for both players during a nervy battle.

Hikaru Nakamura
Levon Aronian
Berlin FIDE Grand Prix 2022
Final – Tiebreak Game 1

position after 40.f4

40...h4+ The easy way to draw was 40...♖d5 and ...♖f5, as White can't make any progress.

41.♔xh4 ♖xf4+ 42.♔g5 ♖f3 43.♔g4 ♖d3 44.♖c5 ♔f6 45.♔f4 ♔e6 46.♔e4

46...♖d8??
This is the pressure of the match-situation. The way to draw was keeping the rook as active as possible with 46...♖h3!, to force White to defend the c3-pawn, so that now 47.♔d4

♖h4+ 48.♔d3 ♖h3+ 49.♔c2 ♖h2+ 50.♔b3 f5! and the running f-pawn holds the draw.

47.♖xb5 ♖d1 48.♖b6+ ♔d7

49.♖f6

The easy win was just pushing the passed pawns with 49.b5! ♖c1 50.♖c6 ♖f1 51.c4, leaving the rook to deal with the f-pawn and the White king to shepherd home the pawns.

49...♔e7 50.♖f3 ♔e6 51.♖d3 f5+ 52.♔d4 ♖b1 53.♖e3+ ♔f6 54.♖e8 f4 55.♖b8?

Correct was 55.♖f8+ ♔g5 56.♔c5!.

55...♔f5 56.b5 f3

57.♔e3?

The winning plan was again 57.♖f8+!, putting the rook behind the passer.

57...♖b3 58.♔d3 ♔g4 59.♔c2

The Berlin GP was decided in a rapid tiebreak game where Hikaru Nakamura kept his sangfroid and Levon Aronian collapsed under the pressure.

59...f2??

A monumental blunder that gifts the win to Nakamura. Correct and drawing was 59...♖a3! 60.♔b2 ♖a5! 61.c4 f2 62.♖f8 ♔g3 63.b6 ♖a6 64.c5 ♖a5! and one of the passed pawns will fall.

60.♖f8 ♖xb5 61.♖xf2

And with the black king cut-off, we reach the famous 'building a bridge' winning Lucena position.

61...♖c5 Black resigned.

There was no comeback for Aronian after that monumental slip-up, and after over-pushing in the second game, Nakamura duly struck again for a resounding 2-0 victory to unexpectedly clinch the Berlin Grand Prix title. With it came the $24,000 first prize and 13 Grand Prix points, while Aronian had to settle for the $18,000 second prize and 10 Grand Prix points.

In victory, a jubilant Nakamura was typically blunt and to the point: 'I am actually proud of the fact that I have not lost a rapid or blitz game for a very, very long time. I think my last loss was probably to Alireza [Firouzja] in 2019. Like I said before, mainly, you just try to find good moves. I think the main difference is that I didn't really feel any pressure. Even today, I was just playing. And I could definitely tell, for Levon, that he was more nervous than I was... In general, I think I played well, and it showed.'

Aronian and Nakamura will now sit out the second leg in Belgrade, but return for the crucial third and final leg back in Berlin. But simply by winning the opening leg, it's wildcard surprise-package Nakamura who moves into pole position in the Grand Prix overall standings. According to the tipsters, he now has a slightly better than 50 percent chance of going forward to the Candidates. ■

The Unstoppable Norwegian

Magnus Carlsen remains the undisputed king of Wijk aan Zee

Having a clear goal and determined to end a two-year drought, Magnus Carlsen set out to win 'his' Tata Steel Masters with an unshakable mindset. There was no stopping him as he defeated the four other Top-10 players and won his 8th trophy with a round to spare. 'Most of my wins were pretty good and pretty clean', was his satisfied conclusion. **DIRK JAN TEN GEUZENDAM** reports from a deserted Wijk aan Zee where the chess was great and the amateurs and spectators were sorely missed.

The return of the Challengers, next to the Masters, doubled the number of players compared to last year. For the 80th edition in 2023 the Tata Steel organizers hope to welcome back the amateurs and spectators as well.

LENNART OOTES

Sometime last summer, Magnus Carlsen found himself thinking about the 2022 Tata Steel Masters. As the thoughts whirred in his head, it occurred to the World Champion that he absolutely had to win. There was no choice. Only first prize in his 15th appearance in the top group would leave him with 'a positive score' of 8 victories out of 15!

And so a highly motivated Norwegian arrived in Wijk aan Zee, determined to wipe out the memory of the last two editions, in which he performed under par and did not win. With a generous supply of leftovers from his preparation for the World Championship match as

Only first prize in his 15th appearance in the top group would leave him with 'a positive score' of 8 victories out of 15!

ammunition, he felt strong. Sticking to a strict schedule and discipline would do the rest.

A further stimulus was his recently expressed wish to take his rating to a totally new level by breaking the 2900 barrier – an ambition that was further proof that Carlsen needs challenges, because they fuel the motivation that brings out the best in him.

The Wimbledon of chess

For Carlsen, 'Wijk aan Zee' is what the Linares tournaments used to be for Garry Kasparov. The 13th World Champion baptized Linares 'The Wimbledon of chess' – a sobriquet now adopted by Wijk aan Zee – and out of the 14 times that he played in the Andalusian town between 1990 and 2005, he finished first 9 times. Linares was Kasparov's tournament to such an extent that he also had a say in its invitation policy and format. Carlsen has no such role in Wijk aan Zee, besides the silent understanding that the players invited will have a respectable average rating.

Carlsen made his debut in Wijk aan Zee in 2004, when he won the 'C Group' and scored his first GM norm. In the morning, he would kick a football with his father on the village green, and in the afternoon he attracted the spectators who had come to see the Masters, to his games. The next two years he played in the Challengers, then prosaically called the 'B Group', before moving to the Masters in 2007. One year later, at the age of 17, he won the Masters for the first time.

Carlsen clearly feels at home in the small Dutch coastal village. First of all, as he has stressed several times, because of its rich chess tradition. But there is more. With his Norwegian liking of the outdoors, he enjoys the walks and runs on the beach and has even tried a wintry dive into the North Sea. And in a way, the simple life of a village without big city distractions makes it easier to focus on one's goal. As he stated afterwards, he lived a disciplined life during the tournament, fully concentrating on his chess and relaxing with exercise and card-playing with his father Henrik and his coach Peter Heine Nielsen in the evenings.

Like anyone else, Carlsen loves Wijk aan Zee when it attracts hundreds of amateurs and spectators, but he also admitted that this time the emptiness of the village helped him focus.

Dubov has to withdraw

Just as last year, Wijk aan Zee felt more like a ghost town than the bustling chess mecca it normally is, where old and new friends traditionally gather around the chess board in the second half of January. The only change was that this time, besides the Masters, the Challengers were back. For the

relatively undramatic. In Round 7, Daniil Dubov forfeited his game against Anish Giri due to 'a Covid infection in his inner circle' and the Russian's refusal to wear a face mask during the game, as he had been requested to do. Dubov did play the next two rounds, but then had to leave the tournament when

It may be called a small miracle that only one player had to withdraw

rest, the measures were actually more stringent than in 2021 because of the high contagiousness of the Omicron variant of the virus. All players and staff were tested at least once a day, and the worries only grew when several staff members tested positive and had to be sent home, while two trainers had to quarantine as well.

In the end, it may be called a small miracle that only one player had to withdraw from the tournament, and that the effect of that withdrawal was

he himself tested positive as well. As a result, he lost his final four games, including his last-round game against Magnus Carlsen. There was a brief period of confusion when, on the day before the final round, it turned out that Dubov (who was quarantining in his hotel room) had tested negative and might play his last game after all. However, that speculation was quickly dispelled, as the provisions of Dutch law in such cases stipulate that the positive test has more weight.

No limousines in Wijk aan Zee for Magnus Carlsen, his coach Peter Heine Nielsen and his father Henrik, but a brisk walk to the venue with the wind whistling in their ears.

But that was much later. Let's return to the early rounds. Magnus Carlsen has the reputation of being a slow starter in Wijk aan Zee, but this time he scored a highly important win as early as Round 2.

NOTES BY
Peter Heine Nielsen

Magnus Carlsen
Anish Giri
Wijk aan Zee 2022 (2)
Catalan Opening, Open Variation

1.d4 ♘f6 2.c4 e6 3.♘f3 d5 4.g3 ♗e7 5.♗g2 0-0 6.0-0 dxc4 7.♘a3?!

Magnus had added the Catalan to his repertoire for the World Championship match, where he played the main move 7.♕c2. With Anish Giri being an expert on the white side as well, it felt natural to try and surprise him with a sub-line, even at the price of it being perhaps somewhat dubious.
7...♗xa3 8.bxa3

8...♗d7

A crucial win as early as Round 2. Magnus Carlsen has played 36.♗e3 and remains at the board, waiting for Anish Giri to resign.

The solid and sensible reply 8...b5 is possible, as 9.a4 can be answered by 9...a6! due to White having doubled pawns on the a-file. White has ways to get decent compensation, but it's not clear who is objectively better.
9.a4!? A very rare continuation.
9...♗c6 10.♗a3 ♖e8 11.♕c2 ♘bd7 12.♖ac1

This is a strange kind of position, in which White can get his pawn back with ♕xc4 – only to immediately lose one again after the reply ...♘b6.
For Black it is not trivial to make a useful move here. 12...♗d5 is met by 13.♖fe1, with e4 to follow, and 12...♘b6 will obviously be poked by

13.a5. The game move, along with 12...a5, is a reasonable choice and leads to a position in which White will be a pawn down – but with sufficient compensation.
12...a6 13.♕xc4 ♘b6 14.♕c3!?
Tempting the knight to take on a4 instead of with the bishop, nudging Black a bit more out of balance.
14...♘xa4 15.♕b3

Again Giri is left with an atypical position to evaluate. Now both 15...♘b6 16.♖xc6 bxc6 17.♘e5 and 15...♗b5 16.♖fe1, followed by 17.e4, obviously leave White with compensation for either the exchange or the pawn. Again, it is not a given that

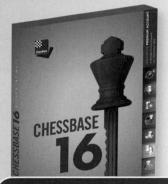
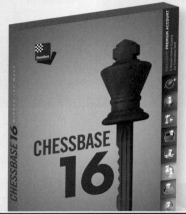

White is objectively better, but from a practical perspective the pressure on Black is considerable.

15...♕d5 16.♖xc6! ♕xc6 17.♘e5 ♕b5 18.♕c2!

Black is a pawn and an exchange up, but the threat of 19.♖b1 still leaves him in a very critical situation. 18...♖eb8 19.♖b1 ♕e8 is the way to restore some coordination while keeping the knight on a4 protected, but after 20.♗xb7 White wins back the pawn and the exchange, retaining a slight edge.

It is, however, possible to cut the Gordian knot with 18...♘b6! 19.♗xb7 ♘c4!, when the tactics work for Black to secure the draw: after 20.♗xa8 ♘xa3 21.♕xc7? ♖xa8 22.♕xf7+ ♔h8 23.♕xe6, 23...♕e8! parries the attack, so White is left with 21.♕c6, when 21...♕xe2 holds the balance.

18...♘d5? 19.♖b1 ♕a5

20.♗xd5?! This is probably enough to keep a winning position, but 20.♗e4! was far cleaner, as after 20...g6 21.♗xd5! White gets a much improved version of the game. The f6-square is weakened but, even more importantly, so is the 7th rank! The

Most of the participants in the Masters stayed in hotel Het Hoge Duin, at a stone's throw from the beach.

main point is that 21...♕xd5 can now be met by 22.♕xc7! b5 23.♕xf7+ ♔h8 24.♖c1!, with an immediate win, since 25.♖c7 is unstoppable. Mate is inevitable.

20...exd5?
Giri thought for quite a while here before making this puzzling mistake. 20...♘xd5 was possible, since 21.♕xc7 b5! 22.♕xf7+ ♔h8 leaves White without an obvious next move to strengthen his attack. So he will have to settle for 21.♕xa4 f6! 22.♘d3 ♕xa2. Similarly, 20...♘c3 also keeps the game going, as after 21.♗b4! ♘xe2+ 22.♕xe2 ♕xd5 23.♖c1 c6 White has the better position in both scenarios, with his two pieces and attacking chances outweighing Black's rook and

two pawns. But Black still very much has chances to defend, especially with the black pawn still on g7!

21.♖xb7

Black's position is worse than it may seem. The threat now is 22. ♗b4, trapping the black queen, and although it can escape via 22...♕e1+, it just means that after 23.♔g2 the a4-knight will lack protection, giving Black no time to defend against the threat on the 7th rank. Giri takes drastic measures, but it is too late.

21...c5 22.♕f5 ♖f8 23.♘xf7 ♕d8 24.dxc5!

Black's problem is that, although he has numerous ways to prevent an immediate mate, they all come at too high a price.

24...♕f6!? 25.♕xf6!
The only winning move, since 25.♕xd5?? ♘c3! would turn the tables to such an extent that it would be White who would have to force the draw with 26.♘h6+ ♔h8 27.♘f7+.
25...gxf6 26.♘h6+ ♔h8 27.c6 ♖fc8 28.c7

Black is doomed to passivity while awaiting the transfer of the white knight to d6.
28...♘c3 29.♗b2 d4 30.♘f7+ ♔g7 31.♘d6

31...♔g6
31...♘xe2+ 32 ♔f1 ♘c3 33 ♗xc3 dxc3 34 ♔e2 also loses trivially.
32.♔f1 ♘b5 33.♘xc8 ♖xc8 34.a4 ♘xc7 35.♗xd4 ♘e6 36.♗e3

And here Giri resigned.

■ ■ ■

This loss was a heavy blow to Anish Giri's aspirations to finally win the Tata Steel Masters after coming so close a couple of times – particularly last year, when he lost a dramatic tie-break against Jorden van Foreest. At first it looked as if his loss to Carlsen had thrown him out of contention, but then two lucky breaks gave him a new lease of life.

His win by default against Dubov in Round 7 was an unexpected windfall, and Fabiano Caruana had given him his first gift one round earlier.

Fabiano Caruana
Anish Giri
Wijk aan Zee 2022 (6)

position after 39...♖e8

It had been a turbulent game, in which both players had held considerable advantages at some point. Now the position would be balanced after the strong 40.♕h5! (which Giri had seen). Instead, Caruana came up with the inexplicable **40.♖b6?** leading to immediate disaster. **40...♘xb6 41.♗xb6 ♗xf5 42.♕xf5 ♗xd4 43.♗xa5 ♗c3 44.♗xc3 ♕xc3**

And with two extra pawns for Black, one of them being a lethal passer on e3, the game was over (0-1, 51).

Pawn power
Apparently, these presents were exactly what the doctor had ordered, as Giri followed up with two excellent wins against Andrey Esipenko and Sam Shankland. Esipenko was submitted to a fine display of pawn power.

NOTES BY
Anish Giri

Andrey Esipenko
Anish Giri
Wijk aan Zee 2022 (8)
Italian Game, Giuoco Pianissimo

1.e4 It is very rare these days to be able to predict even your opponent's first move. Here too, it was hard to guess, since in Wijk aan Zee last year, Andrey Esipenko played 1.d4 against me, which was also a small surprise back then.
1...e5 2.♘f3 ♘c6 3.♗c4
The Italian is a frequent guest in both my and my opponent's practice.
3...♘f6 4.d3 ♗c5 5.c3 0-0 6.0-0

Both sides have many different move orders in the Italian. This particular one allows the ...d5 Italian, which is a fascinating sub-topic within the Italian itself.

6...d5 7.exd5 ♘xd5

There are tons of games and a wealth of analysis revolving around this tabiya. Andrey decides to follow one of the main paths – the trend started by Jorden van Foreest a few years ago and one that earned me some points on the white side as well.

8.♖e1 ♗g4 9.♘bd2 ♘b6 10.h3 ♗h5 11.♘b3

This was the twist back then. White offers a trade of the e5- and d3-pawns.

11...♕xd3 12.♘xe5 ♕f5

The endgame after 12...♗xd1?! is no fun for Black, as I managed to prove in my game against Pentala Harikrishna in the very memorable Shenzhen 2019 tournament (1-0, 40 – see New In Chess 2019/4).

13.♘ef3

Now the pawn structure is rather symmetrical, but the main question is: is White threatening g4 here?

13...♖fe8!?

A rare move, but an option that has

Anish Giri collected his third of four consecutive points thanks to a fine win with the black pieces against Andrey Esipenko.

been around for a while. Most top games go 13...♖ad8, after which grabbing the bishop with 14.g4 is even less attractive, although it does allow 14.♕e2!, grabbing the e-file.

14.g4

Here this is pretty much forced. White has no other way to untangle his pieces.

14...♗xg4 15.hxg4 ♕xg4+ 16.♔h1 ♘e5

A fancy-looking move, but not one I can take creative credit for. It is suggested by the computers and has also been played in a correspondence game.

While Andrey was thinking a little

bit here, I started wondering whether he was contemplating allowing a forced draw with 17.♘xe5 ♕h3+ 18.♔g1 ♕g3+ 19.♔h1. On the one hand, bailing out against a well-prepared opponent is a natural thing to do, but I also suspected he was somewhat familiar with the position, not to mention the fact that playing a double-edged position is in some ways an opportunity.

17.♘h2

This is a winning attempt.

17...♕g6 18.♗c2 ♘d3 19.♗xd3 ♕xd3

Curiously, all this was part of my Chessable course for White. I had no intentions to hide this important sub-variation, plus we are still following the correspondence game. I believe I recommended to not deviate from that game here and follow up with 20.♘b3.

20.♘df3 One of three ways to aim for an endgame, the alternatives being 20.♘b3 and 20.♘df1.

20.♘b3 also led to a fascinating battle, which was eventually drawn: 20...♛xd1 21.♖xd1 ♗xf2 22.♘g4 ♗h4 23.♖g1 (½-½, 51), Rohs (2318)-Larsson (2287), ICCF email 2016.

20...♛xd1 21.♖xd1 ♗xf2

This endgame with three pawns for the piece, in one version or another, was something I had expected to get after playing 13...♖fe8!?. Now it is up to White to mobilize his pieces and conjure up some problems, because if he allows Black to consolidate and trade some material, the three pawns on the kingside will eventually start moving.

22.♗f4 I had expected White to activate his h2-knight with ♘g4, either here or on the next move.

22...c6 23.♖d2?!

Not seeing anything clear-cut, White makes the mistake of allowing trades. Instead, he should have tried to mobilize his minor pieces, probably starting with 23.♘g4, and then try and create some threats on the kingside – although this may be easier said than done.

23...♗e3! As already indicated, trading material kind of helps me.

24.♗xe3 ♖xe3 25.♘d4

Intending to activate the h2-knight. But now I can kick the rook away from the d-file.

25...♘c4!

I was very happy with this move, not only kicking the rook away but also bringing my knight closer to the action.

26.♖f2 ♖ae8

I was getting more and more optimistic. The fact that I can choose to trade a rook at any point with ...♖e1+ was warming my heart.

27.♖af1?! A natural move, but apparently slightly inaccurate.

important how I push my pawns, as my winning chances heavily depend on whether White gets to coordinate his rook and knight to create counterplay.

My initial idea was 31...♖e2+ 32.♔f2 h5, but then I didn't like that after 33.♘f3 I would have to trade the rook before pushing ...g5 in a slightly unfavourable version: 33...♖xf2+ 34.♔xf2 g5 35.a4.

ANALYSIS DIAGRAM

This is smart – creating potential counterplay on the queenside, although even the immediate 35.♖d7+ ♔e7 36.♖d8, followed by ♘d4, seemed to be putting paid to my winning chances. With White's knight solidly centralized and the rook always ready to give checks from behind, I didn't see a realistic way to push my three pawns forward without weakening them too much.

32.♖f2

Anticipating ...♖e2; but now I reverse the move order.

32.♖xh5!? would change the position drastically, but the general outlook would remain the same. White would have to face a long struggle for a

---

The vast Tata Steel complex is only a couple kilometres away from Wijk aan Zee.

27.♘f5 would have led to a better version for White of the same kind of position as in the game. After 27...♖e1+ 28.♖xe1 ♖xe1+ 29.♔g2 we would probably get a similar material balance of rook + knight vs rook, but White mobilizes his pieces for counterplay somewhat faster here.

27...♘d6 I was wondering whether the more ambitious-looking 27...f6 was stronger, but finally decided to go with my instincts and just focus on reducing my opponent's counterchances.

28.♘f5 At first I felt this would make my life easier, but later I was still unsure what the knight trade would do to my winning chances.

28...♘xf5 29.♖xf5

29...f6

There was also some merit in 29...♖8e7!?, intending ...g6 and ...h5 instead, but ...f6 and ...♔f7 felt more natural, and frankly, I didn't doubt too much here.

30.♔g2 ♔f7

Both sides are bringing their king closer to the action. It's not easy for White to come up with a good idea here. Black intends to trade a rook and slowly push the kingside pawns down the board, while White will find it a lot harder to come up with a clear plan.

31.♖d1

31...h5!?

Around here I realized that it is

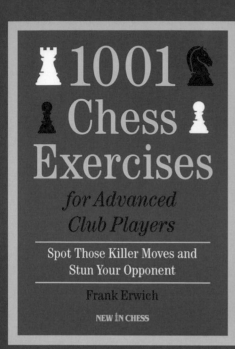
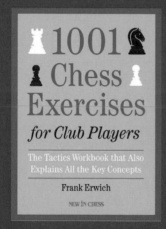

draw. I would enjoy the position after 32...♖e2+ 33.♔g3 ♖xb2 34.♖d7+ ♖e7 35.♖xe7+ ♔xe7 a lot, with two connected passers on the left and a majority on the right. Of course, a draw would still be the most likely outcome here, especially if White defends well.

32...g5! This is good, as I can now meet 33.♘f3 with 33...♔g6!. I thought I could play ...♖e2 later, but looking at the position again, I wonder why I was planning ...♖e2 at all.

33.♖d7+ ♖3e7 34.♖d6 ♖e6 35.♖d7+ ♖8e7!

I can't say I was close to accepting the move repetition, but still, given my low confidence at that point, the fact that I was playing Black, and that I wasn't something like a full rook up at this point, it was not a given that I wouldn't.

36.♖d8

36...g4!?

It wasn't entirely clear to me whether this was a better attempt at pushing for a win than 36...♔g6, but I thought that with the psychological situation and potential time-trouble in mind – with move 40 coming closer but not

quite there yet – this would be a much harder question to answer.

After 36...♔g6 37.♖g8+ ♔g7 38.♖h8 White is hanging on, since it is not easy to push the pawns far up the board, with the rook harassing them from behind.

37.♖h8? A big mistake, and one of the main factors that determined the outcome of this game.

Instead, 37.♘f1! leads to a forcing sequence that works out just fine for White, even though it gets pretty dangerous: 37...h4 (there may be other attempts, but I felt this was the most critical one) 38.♖h8 g3 39.♘f4 ♖e2+ 40.♔g1

ANALYSIS DIAGRAM

(I was hoping that something else would appear here, but the back-up variation that I saw was pretty much the best try anyway) 40...g2 41.♘h2 ♖xb2 42.♖h7+ ♔e8 43.♖xe7+ ♔xe7 44.♖xh4 ♖xa2 45.♖h7+ ♔d6 46.♖xb7 a5. I had a suspicion that this was going to hold for White, which is confirmed by the computers. It's not very comfortable, but since what happened in the game was far more depressing, White clearly should have gone for this.

37...♔g6 38.♖g8+

38...♖g7?

It was a very difficult choice at this point, as frankly both options, this and 38...♔h7, seemed practically losing. Whether White had some hidden defence in either of the two was difficult to see at that point, so I went with the one in which my king is more active. Objectively, this was the wrong call.

Best was 38...♔h7! (it seems that my king's job was to support the pawn mass from up close, on g5, but to guard the rear, covering the h8-g8-f8-squares and neutralizing the white rook on the 8th rank) 39.♖a8 (likewise, 39.♖b8 is met by 39...♖e2, while 39.♖f8 is always met by 39...♔g7!) 39...♖e2, also neutralizing the f2-rook. Now the f-pawn is ready to march (after ...♔g7 if need be). ♘f1 is always met by ...h4!.

39.♖f8 ♔g5

I was very enthusiastic about this, but soon realized that it was not all that easy to actually make progress.

40.♘f1 h4

Preventing the knight from entering the game. 41.♘d2 is met by 41...g3!.

But as the time-control passed and I started thinking about the position more deeply, I realized that it was actually very hard to make progress and that if White just waited and slowly pushed his queenside pawns, there might be no winning this game.

41.a4!

Andrey had come to the same conclusion and realized that he could just start making useful moves on the other side of the board, since my pawns aren't quite rolling yet.

41...a5!

The exclam is for not pushing ...g3, which would have allowed White to liquidate to a drawn rook ending. My first instinct had been 41...♖g6, intending ...♖e5 and ...f5, but the problem is that even after that it's still hard to get the pawns rolling: 42.♖f7 ♖e5 43.♖xb7 f5 44.♖f7

ANALYSIS DIAGRAM

and it's not clear what will come next, since the pawns seem to be stuck. After 41...g3 42.♘xg3! hxg3 43.♔xg3 the rook ending is very drawish, with one extra pawn, as so often, not enough to win.

42.b4

At some point I considered going for the rook ending with 42...g3 43.♘xg3 hxg3, as the c3-pawn is softer thanks to the 41...a5 42.b4 inclusion, but the position still appeared drawn. Instead, I again decided to maintain the tension and hope for the best, although I was not at all sure there would be a win in the end.

42...b6 43.bxa5 I felt this wasn't a good inclusion for White, but it doesn't change too much.

43...bxa5 44.♖a8 ♖e5

White has achieved nothing here and I am ready to push ...f5-f4. It is very tempting now to go for ♘d2-c4, but that turns out to be the losing mistake.

45.♘d2?

White should have continued waiting. Surprisingly, it is still hard for Black to make progress, despite getting the pawn to f5. After 45.♖c8 f5 46.♖f8! White still holds, since there is just no way to push the f-pawn forward.

45...g3!

I had been hoping for this as soon as I went for 41... a5, so it wasn't too hard to clinch the game now.

46.♘f3+ ♔f4

A beautiful idea, stepping into a discovered check, but after 47.♘xe5+ gxf2+! it's a countercheck.

47.♖f1 h3+!

The final sequence.

48.♔xh3 g2 49.♖f2 ♔e3

Setting up a cute finale. White resigned in view of 49...♔e3 50.♖xg2 ♔xf3 51.♖xg7 ♖h5. A pretty mate.

■ ■ ■

Main attraction

Thanks to his four wins in a row, Giri looked fully back in business. After Round 9 he had moved up to second place, only half a point behind Carlsen. The final four rounds of the Tata Steel marathon looked promising for the Dutch number one, but in Round 11 it was again his compatriot Jorden van Foreest who put a damper on his hopes.

Van Foreest faced the tough task of living up to high expectations after last year's sensational win, and the 22-year-old did not disappoint. On the contrary, spoiling for a fight in every game he was probably the most entertaining player in the field. His uncompromising will to do battle resulted in four wins and four losses and words of praise from Magnus Carlsen, on whose team he had been working before and during the match in Dubai. Carlsen could barely suppress his enthusiasm: 'What can you say? For me, both as a player and as a spectator, his games have been pretty much the main attraction. It's been great to see.' Van Foreest's win against Giri made Carlsen's life easier, but it was also the best game Van Foreest played.

NOTES BY
Jorden van Foreest

**Jorden van Foreest
Anish Giri**
Wijk aan Zee 2022 (11)
Nimzo-Indian Defence, Sämisch Variation

**1.d4 ♘f6 2.c4 e6 3.♘c3 ♗b4
4.a3**

Jorden van Foreest scored his finest victory in the Dutch duel with Anish Giri.

Since this game was played after a rest day, I had a lot of time to prepare. When I play Anish Giri, I am usually not too sure what to play, and all sorts of crazy ideas passed through my mind before I finally hit upon the Sämisch Variation of the Nimzo-Indian.

I have always been fascinated by this line, but had never played it in a classical game before. The variation is very complex, and White risks a lot right from the start by voluntarily allowing the doubling of his pawns on the c-file. In return, his hopes lie in trying to get dynamic play by using his central pawns and the bishop pair.
4...♗xc3+ 5.bxc3 b6
Here 5...c5 and 5...♘c6 are the other main moves. In general, all three moves are based on the same concept,

Spoiling for a fight in every game, Jorden van Foreest was probably the most entertaining player in the field

viz. that Black tries to attack the feeble white c4-pawn as quickly and as persistently many times as he can.

6.f3 Preparing to increase the central control by going e2-e4.

6...♘c6 Black could stop White from playing e2-e4 by going 6...d5 instead, but that would immediately free White from his structural weak-nesses. Instead, he intends to bring his knight to a5, from where it will put pressure on c4.

7.e4 ♘a5 8.♗d3 ♗a6 9.♕e2

9...d6?! Not the most accurate move. Anish later told me that he had mixed up his lines.
9...c5 is more accurate, followed by bringing the rook to the c-file, adding even more pressure to c4.
10.f4! Intending to develop the knight to f3. The white pawn centre starts looking daunting now.
10...♕d7?!
A typical idea in this type of position, planning to bring out the queen to a4. In this specific case, this plan is too slow and the pieces on the queenside will be out of play.
Interestingly, the counter-intuitive

10...d5 is the computer suggestion, breaking open the white centre, even at the cost of a pawn.

11.♘f3 ♕a4

12.♘d2 Defending just in time. In fact, 12.e5 would have been even more accurate, stopping Black's next move.

12...e5! A good defensive idea, blocking the centre before White gets the chance to go e5 himself.

13.0-0

13...0-0!?

My first reaction to this move was absolute shock. I thought it was suicidal and had only considered queenside castling for Black. Surely, an exchange sac with ♖xf6 should be winning now, right? However, the longer I looked, the less sure I became.

I figured that after 13...0-0-0 14.♖b1 my opponent did not like his prospects, since his king will be exposed forever.

14.fxe5 After thinking for about 15 minutes, I decided that this was the way to go, although I was not sure of anything yet.

14...dxe5

My first reaction was absolute shock. I thought this move was suicidal

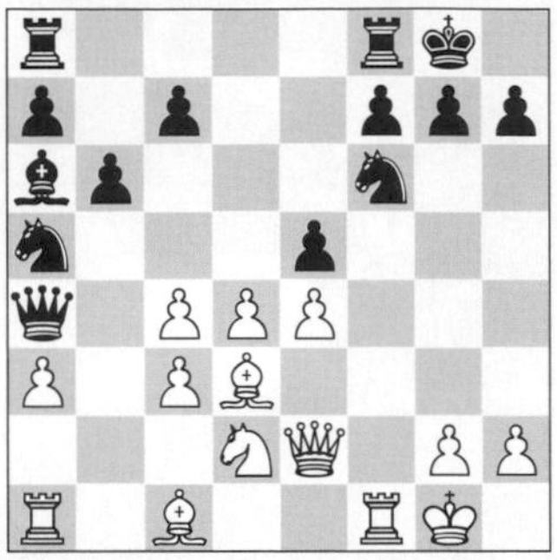

15.♖b1 Having spent oceans of time on 15.♖xf6 and not finding anything clear, I finally decided on the text-move. It was only after the game that I discovered that sacrificing on f6 would in fact have been crushing, even here. After 15.♖xf6 gxf6, 16.♕f2 is the winning move, but I did not know what to do after either 16...♕c6 or, more importantly, my main worry 16...♕d1+, since I did not see a convenient way to parry the check (after 16...♕c6 White has 17.a4! to bring the bishop into the game via a3. I had been so fixated on getting it to h6 that this idea had escaped my attention). I had seen 17.♘f1!, but thought it would just leave my bishop en prise (after 17.♗f1 ♕g4 Black is doing fine, now that the queen has magically appeared on the kingside to aid in the defence), and I stopped my calculations after 17...♕xd3,

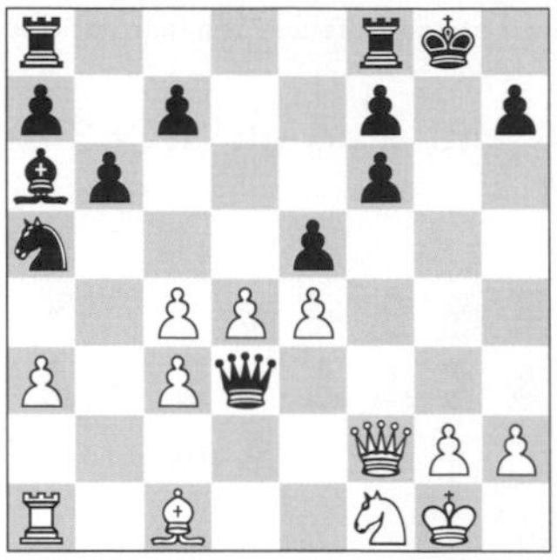

ANALYSIS DIAGRAM

not seeing a way to continue the attack. But now 18.♕h4!! is a beautiful move, cutting off the black queen from the defence. Strangely enough, Black is completely helpless against the idea of ♗h6, followed by a swift mate. 18...♗b7 19.d5!, and Black is lost.

Wijk aan Zee 2022 Masters

					1	2	3	4	5	6	7	8	9	10	11	12	13	14		TPR
1	Magnus Carlsen	IGM	NOR	2865	*	1	1	1	½	½	½	1	½	½	½	1	½	1	9½	2902
2	Shakhriyar Mamedyarov	IGM	AZE	2767	0	*	½	½	½	1	½	½	1	1	½	1	½	½	8	2821
3	Richard Rapport	IGM	HUN	2763	0	½	*	½	½	1	½	1	0	½	½	1	1	1	8	2821
4	Anish Giri	IGM	NED	2772	0	½	½	*	½	0	1	1	½	½	1	½	½	1	7½	2791
5	Sergey Karjakin	IGM	RUS	2743	½	½	½	½	*	1	0	½	½	1	0	1	½	½	7	2765
6	Jorden van Foreest	IGM	NED	2702	½	0	0	1	0	*	0	½	½	1	1	1	1	½	7	2768
7	Andrey Esipenko	IGM	RUS	2714	½	½	½	0	1	1	*	½	½	½	½	0	½	½	6½	2738
8	Fabiano Caruana	IGM	USA	2792	0	½	0	0	½	½	½	*	1	½	½	1	1	½	6½	2732
9	Jan-Krzysztof Duda	IGM	POL	2760	½	0	1	½	½	½	½	0	*	½	½	½	½	½	6	2706
10	Vidit Gujrathi	IGM	IND	2727	½	0	½	½	0	0	½	½	½	*	1	0	1	1	6	2708
11	Sam Shankland	IGM	USA	2708	½	½	½	0	1	0	½	½	½	0	*	½	½	½	5½	2682
12	R. Praggnanandhaa	IGM	IND	2612	0	0	0	½	0	0	1	0	½	1	½	*	1	1	5½	2689
13	Nils Grandelius	IGM	SWE	2672	½	½	0	½	½	0	½	0	½	0	½	0	*	1	4½	2631
14	Daniil Dubov	IGM	RUS	2720	0	½	0	0	½	½	½	½	½	0	½	0	0	*	3½	2563

15...c5? A real mistake, depriving Black of the much needed counterplay. Now, going for the exchange sacrifice became a much simpler decision. 15...♖ae8! was called for, with a completely unclear position.
16.♖xf6! 16.d5? would be a huge error after 16...♘e8!.
16...gxf6

17.♕f3 The engines show 17.♘b3 as more accurate. I had not seen that move at all ☺. Fortunately, the text is good, too.
17.♕f2 doesn't work that well right now, as the rook on b1 is sidelined after 17...♕d1+ 18.♔f1 ♕xd3.
17...♕c6 18.d5!

Cutting the position in half. Black is deprived of all counterplay and his queenside pieces are left as spectators to the action.
It is important to note that with the black pawn still on c7, there would have been the nasty 18...♕c5+, which would have made all the difference.
18...♕d6 19.♘f1 The white position is playing itself. All forces will be brought to the kingside.
19...♔h8 20.♘e3 ♗c8 21.♗d2
To transfer the bishop to h4.

21...♖g8 Here 21...♘b7 might have been a better defence. Bringing the knight to d6 quickly is paramount. 22.♖f1 ♕e7 23.d6!. Clearing d5 for the knight, but even so it's not clear whether White is winning after 23...♕e6!. A nice defence is shown in the following line: 24.♘d5 ♖g8! 25.♘c7 ♕xd6 26.♘xa8 ♗g4! 27.♕e3 ♖xa8, and Black is still hanging on, albeit only by a thread.
22.♗e1 ♖g6

23.♗h4 Interesting would have been 23.h4, to kick away the rook: 23...♗d7 24.h5 ♖g5 25.♗h4 ♖ag8, but still Black retains chances of a successful defence.
23...♖h6?!
I had missed this move. I briefly worried that I had to make what looked like an awkward defensive move with 24.♕f2. As it turns out, however, the rook move plays into White's hands, as it clears the way for the idea of ♗e2-g4, exchanging the light-squared bishops and getting access to f5 for the knight. A good defensive try was 23...♗d7, often intending to put a pawn on h5 and not allowing the bishop swap. Still, after extensive analysis, I have still not found a way for Black to save the game after the following moves, which seem to be the best line of play: 24.♕f2! h5 25.♗e2 ♖h6 26.♖f1 ♘b7 27.a4!.

ANALYSIS DIAGRAM

The key-move, soon to allow White to open a second front with a4-a5.
24.♕f2 ♗d7 25.♖f1

25...♔g7 The rest is quite straightforward. It would have been more resilient to bait White into taking on f6: 25...♘b7. Now, if White were to take on f6, things would not be so simple: 26.♗xf6+ ♕xf6 27.♕xf6+ ♖xf6 28.♖xf6 ♔g7 would give Black good chances of defence. However, White is by no means forced to do this. He can just proceed with his plans: 26.♗e2! ♖g8, and now 27.♗h5! is a nice point.

ANALYSIS DIAGRAM

26.♗e2!
Now the bishop joins in and the king on g7 will be in the midst of things.

26...♖g6
A clever idea, but it's not enough.

27.h3!
27.♗h5 ♖f8 was the idea, although here, too, h3 is winning.

27...♗xh3

28.♗h5
Now Black is not in time to defend with ...♖f8, as the bishop will be left hanging. So his entire structure collapses.
For a second I considered the pretty 28.♕f5, only to realize that Black has the counter-trick 28...♖xg2+. One always has to remain careful!

28...♗d7 29.♗xg6 fxg6 30.♗xf6+ ♔g8

At this point, the position was just too good to mess up, even though Anish kept fighting well and throwing obstacles in my way.

31.♕h4 ♖f8 32.♖f3 ♖f7 33.♕g5 ♕f8 34.♕xe5 ♘b7 35.♕f4 ♘d6 36.e5 ♘e8 37.d6
Giving some life to the black bishop, but the white knight entering via d5 or g4 is more relevant.

37...♘xf6 38.exf6 ♕e8 39.♘d5 ♕e1+ 40.♔h2 ♕d1 41.♘e7+ ♔h8 42.♖h3!
A nice final touch, as 42...♗xh3 runs into 43.d7, followed by ♕b8+ and mate.
I am very pleased with this win – definitely my best of the tournament.

■ ■ ■

'Absurdly well'

The main difference between the Carlsen in Wijk aan Zee of the past two years and this one was that he created chances in abundance – and was converting them. By his own calculation, he had had nine winning positions and converted five. There could probably have been one or two more, but it still left him with a feeling of satisfaction. Clearly his best win was the game against Shakhriyar Mamedyarov, a win that was partly thanks to Daniil Dubov, who had helped him overcome his fear of sacrificing pawns in the Catalan during his preparation for the world championship match.

Carlsen's beautiful win elicited unaccustomed praise from the loser, who combined disbelief and admiration when he pronounced it his favourite game in the tournament, saying: 'He played absolutely brilliantly. Before the tournament I thought that humans stand no chance against the engines, but now I think there may be a chance, because Magnus played absurdly well. A fantastic game. I believe that 25 of the 27 moves were the computer's first choice. I can't remember ever losing like this. I had no chance. This was the best game.'

NOTES BY
Peter Heine Nielsen

Magnus Carlsen
Shakhriyar Mamedyarov
Wijk aan Zee 2022 (9)
Catalan Opening

1.d4 ♘f6 2.♘f3 d5 3.c4 e6 4.g3 dxc4 5.♗g2 ♗b4+ 6.♗d2 a5

This may be a sub-line against the Catalan, but it is a respectable one that was used by Veselin Topalov in his World Championship matches against both Vladimir Kramnik and Vishy Anand.
For Magnus it may have stirred bad memories, since he lost with the white pieces in this line against that same Kramnik in Wijk aan Zee back in 2010. That time, he tried the rare 7.♘c3, but now 7.♕c2 has been accepted as the main continuation.

7.0-0 0-0 8.e3?!

While 7.0-0 is still seen as quite respectable, this is considered dubious. When Shakhriyar Mamedyarov praised Magnus at the closing ceremony for playing like a computer, he highlighted 8.e3 as the exception!

Just as in the game against Anish Giri, this initiates a sequence in which it's hard to say who is objectively better. However, from a practical point of view, it is White who has the fun of attacking his opponent's king!

8...♖a6!? Numerous moves are possible here, but this one is praised by the computer, and it is likely that Mamedyarov recalled it from his preparation. Black now keeps his extra pawn and secures the long diagonal, **9.♕c2 b5 10.a4 c6 11.♘c3 ♖b6 12.e4**

White threatens 13. e5, followed by 14.♘g5, provoking ...g6, which would severely weaken the dark squares around the black king. Mamedyarov's move is therefore logical, but the engines insist that 12...h6 is critical. And it's true that White will have to prove now that his kingside attack is justified. White has numerous tries – 13.e5, followed by 14.♕e4, being the most obvious one.

12...♗e7 13.e5 ♘d5 Black's idea is that after 14.♘xd5 cxd5 15.♗xa5 b4 his compensation for the exchange is obvious. The computer claims that after 16.♗xb6 ♕xb6 17.a5! ♕a7 18.b3! White can still hope for an edge, but he is clearly taking a strategic risk and has a much weaker version of the exchange sacrifice than in the game. **14.axb5**

14...cxb5?!
A bad decision in hindsight, but one that might have won you the game if your opponent had not been Magnus. Mamedyarov insists on sacrificing the exchange, leaving White no other option than to accept.

14...♘b4!? was the computer's way of doing it, with 15.♕e4 cxb5 16.♕g4 f5!? being the plan, with an unclear position assessed as equal by the machines.

15.♘xd5 exd5 16.♗xa5 ♘c6 17.♗xb6 ♕xb6

Black's compensation is very visible. White has a weak pawn on d4 and Black is set up well to attack it, with ...♗g4 coming next, undermining the vital defender. At the same time, ...b4 will almost guarantee that Black gets a passed pawn on the queenside. Add the bishop pair, and Black's compensation indeed seems more than sufficient.

18.♖a8!
This game is decided on moves 18 and 19, and when Mamedyarov talks about Magnus playing like a computer, it boils down to this sequence, which shows he understands the position better than his opponent.

The general factors in the position as described previously are not unfavourable for Black, so White needs to catch him while he is still unbalanced. Mamedyarov continues making logical moves, but the position, despite the play having slowed down after a tactical sequence, hangs on very concrete specifics.

That urgency was required from

WHY IS IT THAT MAGNUS FEELS AT HOME SO MUCH IN WIJK AAN ZEE?

THE ANSWER MY FRIEND, IS BLOWING IN THE WIND

BEREND VONK

Magnus Carlsen's favourite tournament

Many champions seem to have a tournament where they perform better. For Garry Kasparov, it was Linares, which he won nine times. For Vladimir Kramnik, it was the Dortmund Sparkassen Chess Meeting, where he was a ten-time winner.

For Magnus Carlsen, it is undoubtedly the annual tournament at Wijk aan Zee, the Netherlands, which since 2011 has been named for Tata Steel, the tournament's sponsor.

Carlsen made his breakthrough on the international stage in Wijk aan Zee in 2004 as a 13-year-old when he swept to victory in the C group,

securing his first grandmaster norm. Two years later, he won the B group, thereby elevating himself to the elite, or A group, the following year. He has played there every year since, except in 2014, winning the tournament a total of eight times, including this year's edition. Carlsen has not only won the tournament more than anyone else in the event's history, which goes back to 1938, he is ascending the lists of the people who have played and won the most games there. The following is an overview of Carlsen's career at Wijk aan Zee.

DYLAN LOEB McCLAIN

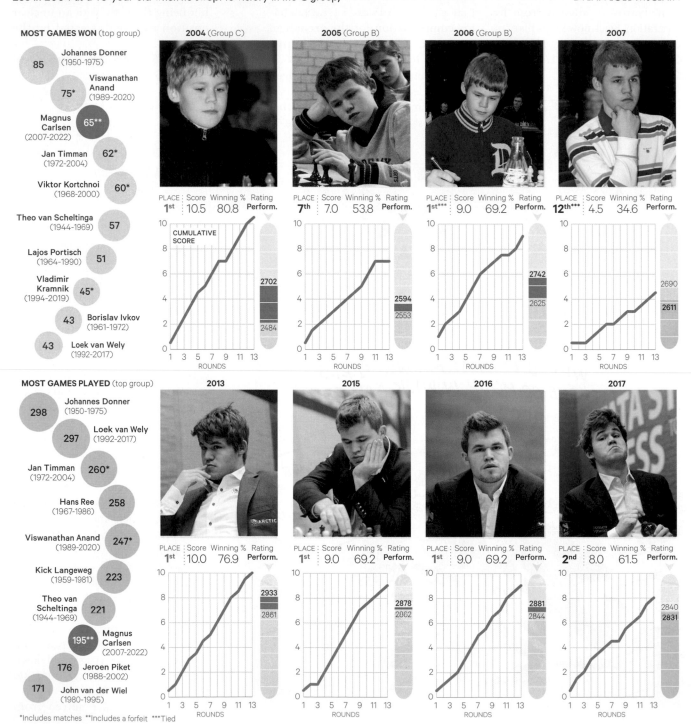

MOST GAMES WON (top group)

85	Johannes Donner (1950-1975)
75*	Viswanathan Anand (1989-2020)
65**	Magnus Carlsen (2007-2022)
62*	Jan Timman (1972-2004)
60*	Viktor Kortchnoi (1968-2000)
57	Theo van Scheltinga (1944-1969)
51	Lajos Portisch (1964-1990)
45*	Vladimir Kramnik (1994-2019)
43	Borislav Ivkov (1961-1972)
43	Loek van Wely (1992-2017)

2004 (Group C)
PLACE **1st** · Score 10.5 · Winning % 80.8 · Rating Perform.
CUMULATIVE SCORE — 2702 / 2484

2005 (Group B)
PLACE **7th** · Score 7.0 · Winning % 53.8 · Rating Perform.
2594 / 2553

2006 (Group B)
PLACE **1st*** · Score 9.0 · Winning % 69.2 · Rating Perform.
2742 / 2625

2007
PLACE **12th*** · Score 4.5 · Winning % 34.6 · Rating Perform.
2690 / 2611

MOST GAMES PLAYED (top group)

298	Johannes Donner (1950-1975)
297	Loek van Wely (1992-2017)
260*	Jan Timman (1972-2004)
258	Hans Ree (1967-1986)
247*	Viswanathan Anand (1989-2020)
223	Kick Langeweg (1959-1981)
221	Theo van Scheltinga (1944-1969)
195**	Magnus Carlsen (2007-2022)
176	Jeroen Piket (1988-2002)
171	John van der Wiel (1980-1995)

2013
PLACE **1st** · Score 10.0 · Winning % 76.9 · Rating Perform.
2933 / 2861

2015
PLACE **1st** · Score 9.0 · Winning % 69.2 · Rating Perform.
2878 / 2062

2016
PLACE **1st** · Score 9.0 · Winning % 69.2 · Rating Perform.
2881 / 2844

2017
PLACE **2nd** · Score 8.0 · Winning % 61.5 · Rating Perform.
2840 / 2831

*Includes matches **Includes a forfeit ***Tied

MOST TOURNAMENTS WON (top group, includes ties)

8	Viswanathan Anand (1989, 1998, 2003, 2004, 2006)	Max Euwe (1940, 1942, 1952, 1958)	Levon Aronian (2007, 2008, 2012, 2014)	Viktor Kortchnoi (1968, 1971, 1984, 1987)	Lajos Portisch (1965, 1972, 1975, 1978)	Johannes Donner (1950, 1958, 1963)	Efim Geller (1965, 1969, 1977)	Garry Kasparov (1999, 2000, 2001)	John Nunn (1982, 1990, 1991)
Magnus Carlsen (2008, 2010, 2013, 2015, 2016, 2018, 2019, 2022)	5	4	4	4	4	3	3	3	3

2008

PLACE	Score	Winning %	Rating Perform.
1st***	8.0	61.5	2830 / 2733

2009

PLACE	Score	Winning %	Rating Perform.
5th***	7.0	53.8	2776 / 2740

2010

PLACE	Score	Winning %	Rating Perform.
1st	8.5	65.4	2822 / 2810

2011

PLACE	Score	Winning %	Rating Perform.
3rd***	8.0	61.5	2821 / 2814

2012

PLACE	Score	Winning %	Rating Perform.
2nd***	8.0	61.5	2835 / 2835

2018

PLACE	Score	Winning %	Rating Perform.
1st***	9.0	69.2	2885 / 2834

2019

PLACE	Score	Winning %	Rating Perform.
1st	9.0	69.2	2888 / 2835

2020

PLACE	Score	Winning %	Rating Perform.
2nd	8.0	61.5	2872 / 2818

2021

PLACE	Score	Winning %	Rating Perform.
6th	7.5	57.7	2872 / 2771

2022

PLACE	Score	Winning %	Rating Perform.
1st	9.5	73.1	2902 / 2865

White is illustrated by the fact that after 18.h3 (preventing ...♗g4) 18...♗e6 Black already has a pleasant position.

18...h6?

A very logical move. 18...♗e6 would have allowed 19.♖xf8+ ♗xf8 20.♘g5, attacking the e6-bishop and threatening mate on h7. Mamedyarov probably stopped calculating here, but after 20...g6 Black's position is actually fine, since White has no logical follow-up, so the pawn on d4 will fall.

Similarly, 18...b4 intending ...b3! and fixing the pawn structure just in time, would also have given Black decent counterplay.

19.♖fa1

A good move. Whether 19.♖xc8!? ♖xc8 20.♕f5, followed by 21.e6, was even better is more of a philosophical question, since both moves leave White with a considerable edge.

19...♗e6?

Another very logical-looking move, after which the position is completely lost!

Black's absolutely last chance was to play 19...b4 intending 20... b3. Black

At the prize-giving Shakhriyar Mamedyarov got everyone laughing, including Tata Steel Netherlands CEO Hans van den Berg, as he waxed lyrical about the game he lost to Magnus Carlsen.

exploits the fact that after 20.b3, 20...♘xd4! is possible, with 21.♘xd4 ♕xd4 22.♖d1 ♗f5! being the point.

20.♕d1!

As innocent-looking as it gets, but crushing. White first coordinated his defences and managed to double on the a-file, before withdrawing his queen.

20...b4

This forces matters, but as White is in time to defend, it just makes things worse for Black. But Black has no other reasonable moves. He has to keep attacking d4 to prevent White from regrouping with ♘e1-c2.

21.b3! c3 22.♖8a6!

Forcing the queen away from attacking d4.

22...♕c7 23.♘e1!

Two key aims have been achieved: Black's passed pawn has been solidly blocked, and the knight has been released of its defensive duties and can now be rerouted to e3.

23...f6?!

Making things worse; but Black's position was beyond repair anyway.

24.♘d3! fxe5 25.♘xe5 ♘xe5 26.♖xe6! c2 27.♕e1

And since 27...♘d3 28.♖xe7 wins easily for White, Mamedyarov resigned.

■ ■ ■

Consummate ease

At 36, Mamedyarov was the oldest participant in the Masters, which made him exclaim at the prizegiving: 'Vishy, where are you?' Over the years, Mamedyarov has been an unpredictable force in Wijk aan Zee, alternating brilliancies with short, insipid draws or worse. This time, he was in good shape and one of the darlings of the online audience. Here is one of his wins, which shows the consummate ease with which he can handle complicated positions.

NOTES BY
Shakhriyar Mamedyarov

Jorden van Foreest
Shakhriyar Mamedyarov
Wijk aan Zee 2022 (5)
Ruy Lopez, Open Variation

1.e4 e5 2.♘f3 ♘c6 3.♗b5 a6 4.♗a4 ♘f6 5.0-0 ♘xe4 6.d4 b5 7.♗b3 d5 8.dxe5 ♗e6 9.a4!?

A relatively rare and surprising move in this position of the Open Ruy Lopez. As a result I had to spend time

At 36, Mamedyarov was the oldest participant in the Masters, which made him exclaim: 'Vishy, where are you?'

here. Far more common are 9.c3 and 9.♘bd2, wile 9.♕e2 and 9.♗e3 are also played more often.

9...b4 10.♗e3 ♗e7 11.a5 0-0 12.♕d3 ♘c5 13.♗xc5 ♗xc5 14.c3

My opponent played all his opening moves fast.

14...♘e7 Also interesting was 14...g6!?, when White can continue with 15.h4, but Black is fine.

15.♘bd2 bxc3 16.bxc3 ♗a7 17.♘d4

17...♗d7 Perhaps stronger was withdrawing the bishop all the way: 17...♗c8!? 18.♗c2 g6 19.♕e3 c5 20.♕h6 (after 20.♘4f3 ♘f5 21.♕f4 the point of withdrawing the bishop to c8 becomes clear, as Black can now play 21...f6! 22.♖ad1 fxe5 23.♕xe5 ♗b8) 20...cxd4 21.♘f3 ♘f5 22.♗xf5 ♗xf5 23.♘g5

ANALYSIS DIAGRAM

23...♕xg5!! (this was the idea!) 24.♕xg5 dxc3, and Black has good play, despite his slight material deficit.

18.♘2f3?! I think this was the start of a miscalculation on his part.

To my mind, he needed to play 18.♗c2!, and now the play could continue 18...g6 19.♕e3 c5 20.♘4f3 ♘f5 21.♗xf5 (21.♕f4 would be

Shakhriyar Mamedyarov (36), the oldest participant in the Masters, in the process of punishing a miscalculation by Jorden van Foreest.

LENNART OOTES

26...♗c5? This loses a large part of the advantage. Black would be winning after 26...♘e4! 27.♗d3 ♕e7, but I felt that the white a-pawn was a dangerous and wanted to eliminate it. **27.♗d3 ♖xa5 28.♖xa5 ♕xa5 29.h4**

29...h5?! And here 29...g6! was better. **30.g3! ♘e8?!** I wanted to reroute the knight to f6, but had missed his very strong reply. That reply I could have prevented by playing 30...♕c7!.

31.c4! dxc4 Interesting was 31...♘f6!? 32.cxd5 ♗xd5 33.♕f4! ♔h8, with a complicated position. **32.♗h7+ ♔f8 33.♗g6 ♘f6 34.♗xf7 ♔xf7**

tempting here, since after 21... f6 – 21...c4 would have been stronger – 22.♖fe1 ♗b8 23.♘b3 fxe5 24.♕d2! my bishop is not on c8 and d5 is not protected) 21...♗xf5 22.♕h6 f6!, and Black is OK.
18...c5 19.e6 ♗e8 20.♘g5
Here 20.♗c2 f5 21.♘e2 ♗b8 would lead to a very unclear position.
20...f5!

21.♘f7? I think he had calculated this far, but had missed my reply. A better chance for White was 21.♕h3!? h6 22.♘f7 ♗xf7 23.exf7+ ♖xf7 24.♘e6 ♕d6 25.♖ae1, when White has some compensation for the pawn.

21...♖xf7! Very strong. Black wins material. **22.exf7+ ♗xf7**

The knight is hanging and Black is threatening the fork ...c4.
23.♘xf5 c4 24.♗xc4 ♘xf5 25.♗xa6 ♘d6 26.♕f3

35.♖c1? A losing mistake. Unfortunately for him, he hadn't seen how White could escape here: 35.♕b7+! ♔g8 (since after 35...♗e7 36.♖c1 ♕c5 White would have

ANALYSIS DIAGRAM

37.♕f3!!, with an unbelievable zugzwang and a draw: 37...♔g6 – 37...♗d6 38.♕c3! – 38.♕e2 c3 39.♕d3+ ♔f7 40.♕xc3 with a draw) 36.♕c8† ♔h7 37.♕f5† ♔g8, and it's a draw.
35...♕c7!

Now Black is winning.
36.♔g2 ♗d4 37.♕a8 c3 38.♕a2+ ♔g6 39.♕c2+ ♔h6 40.♕d3 ♕b7+ 41.f3 ♕b2+ 42.♖c2 ♕b1 43.♕f5 ♗e3 44.♔h3 ♕d1!

Indirectly covering the c-pawn and leaving White with a hopeless position, so he resigned. An important and interesting win for me with the black pieces against last year's winner!

'Just flawless'
In the final standings, Mamedyarov shared second place with Richard Rapport. The Hungarian continued to impress with the imaginative chess that has made him a top-10 player, but he also continued to criticize his own play. Typical was his comment at the prize-giving when asked to name his favourite game. He immediately chose his win by default against Dubov, adding 'just flawless'. Needless to say, there were games that deserved more attention.

NOTES BY
Jan Timman

**Fabiano Caruana
Richard Rapport**
Wijk aan Zee 2022 (10)
English Opening, Mikenas-Carls Variation

1.c4 e6 2.♘c3 ♘f6 3.e4 c5 4.e5 ♘g8 5.d4 cxd4 6.♕xd4 ♘c6

7.♕f4
More usual is 7.♕e4, but practice has shown that White has no realistic chances of an opening advantage, mainly because Black will be able to develop his king's knight to f6 with tempo.

The text was first played in the game Hu-Booth from the 2008 Australian championship. Two years ago, Dubov introduced it in grandmaster practice

> **Richard Rapport continued to impress with the imaginative chess that has made him a top-10 player, but he also continued to criticize his own play**

against Kovalev – also in Wijk aan Zee. Esipenko has also played this twice.
7...d6 8.♘f3

8...♘h6!
Kovalev developed his knight with 8...♘ge7, but this wastes valuable time. After 9.exd6 ♘g6 10.♕e4 ♕xd6 11.♗d2 ♗e7 12.0-0-0 White was clearly better. The text is stronger, because it gives White very little chance to create an initiative.
Esipenko-Krejci, Prague 2021, saw 8...dxe5, but that's a concession. After 9.♘xe5 ♘f6 10.♘xc6 bxc6 11.♕f3 ♗b7 12.♗f4 White was clearly better.
9.exd6 In Dubov-Pichot, Crypto Cup 2021, White went for the developing move 9.♗d2, but Black had few problems after 9...dxe5 10.♘xe5 ♗d6 11.♘xc6 ♗xf4 12.♘xd8 ♗xd2+ 13.♔xd2 ♔xd8 14.♗d3 ♔e7.

Richard Rapport finished shared second and defeated Fabiano Caruana, but not for the first time the Hungarian found it hard to be happy with his play.

Caruana probably didn't like this, but the text doesn't look like an improvement for White.

9...♗xd6 10.♕g5 ♕xg5

I'm not sure what Caruana had planned after 10...0-0. The black position looks good, and the computer is inclined to indicate a slight plus for Black.

11.♗xg5

11...f5 An interesting continuation – Black vacates square f7 for his knight, keeping the white king's knight from e4. The alternative was 11...♘f5, also with an acceptable position.

12.0-0-0 ♗c5!

The best move, since 12...♘f7 would be met by 13.♗e3, giving White an advantage. White controls square c5, and 13...f4 will be met strongly by the simple 14.♗d2, giving White the important central square e4 for his knight.

13.♘e5 Forcing a slight weakening of Black's queenside. But White will also have to concede a weakening. The alternative was 13.♗h4, which could be followed by 13...♘g4 14.♖d2 h6 15.h3 ♘f6 16.♗xf6 gxf6 17.a3 a5 18.♘a4 b6, and the position is equal.

13...♘f7 14.♘xc6 bxc6 15.♗e3 ♗xe3+ 16.fxe3 ♔e7 17.♗e2 g5

The alternative was 17...e5, but Rapport wants to reserve square e5 for his rook and to create space on the kingside.

18.♘a4

White is going to put his knight on the vital c5-square. With 18.h4 g4 19.e4 he could have mended the weakness of his e-pawn, but this won't yield him an advantage either, e.g. 19...♘e5 20.♖hf1 ♖f8 21.g3 a5 22.♘a4 h5, and the chances are roughly equal.

18...h5 19.♘c5 h4 20.g4

The correct way to keep sufficient space on the kingside.

20...♘e5

21.♖d4 Caruana was clearly off form. This is a bad miscalculation. Correct was the natural 21.♖hg1. White needn't worry about his c-pawn. After 21...fxg4 22.♗xg4 ♘xc4 23.♗e2 ♘xe3 24.♖d3 ♘d5 25.♖xg5 he has sufficient positional compensation for the pawn.

21...♘xg4 22.♗xg4

22...e5

Caruana must have missed this intermediate move. This is another confirmation of my theory about blunders: when you're tired, you may overlook in your calculations that a piece has left a square. In this case, there was a knight on e5, so the square *seemed* unavailable.

23.♖d2 fxg4 24.♘d3

White's best chance. The knight is aiming for e5.

24...♖h6 The computer strongly prefers 24...♗f5, intending to meet 25.♘xe5 with 25...♔e6, after which the main line continues as follows: 26.♘xc6 ♗e4 27.♘d4+ ♔e5 28.♖g1 g3 29.hxg3 h3 30.♖h2 g4, and the white h2-rook has been surrounded.

ANALYSIS DIAGRAM

The computer assesses this position as winning – but is it really that simple? White has a kind of fortress. The text has the advantage that it keeps the battle field open.

25.♘xe5 ♖e6 26.♘xg4 ♖e4

The point of the previous moves. Black has sacrificed two pawns, and now regains one while maintaining his initiative.

27.♘f2 ♖xc4+ 28.♔c2

With 28.♔d1 White could have kept all the rooks on the board. After 28...♗e6 29.♖g1 ♖g8 30.b3 ♖c5 31.h3 he has a reasonably solid defensive line, but Black obviously still has winning chances.

28...♖xc2+ 29.♔xc2 ♗e6 30.♖g1 ♖f8 31.♘d3 g4

32.♘f4 32.♔c3 would have left the option of where to put the white knight open. Maybe Caruana feared 32...♖f3, but then he has 33.♔d4. The white king is relatively safe in the middle. After 33...♖h3 34.♖g2 g3 35.hxg3 ♖xg3 36.♖h2 h3 37.♘f4 White would be able to hold for the moment, but the defence would continue to be an uphill struggle.

32...♗f5+ 33.♔d2 ♖d8+

34.♔e2 It seems obvious to move the king to the threatened flank, but 34.♔c3 would have been a better defence. After 34...♔f6 35.e4 ♗c8 36.♘d3 Black would find it hard to make progress.

34...♔f6 35.b3 More tenacious was 35.b4, conquering space on the queenside. But Black is already winning, although accurate play is still required. Remarkably enough, White will be in zugzwang after 35...♖d7 36.a3 a6!. Knight and king have no squares, and 37.♖c1 will be met decisively by 37...♗e4.

35...a5!

Rapport plays very powerfully in this final stage of the game. The text is the computer's first move, underlining White's powerlessness. White is constricted even further.

36.♔e1 ♔e5 37.♘g2 ♖h8 38.♘f4 g3 Time for the decisive breakthrough. **39.♖g2**

After 39.hxg3 h3 White would have to give a piece for the h-pawn.

39...♗e4 40.♖d2 h3 41.a3 ♖d8!

A hammer blow. White cannot take the rook.

42.♖b2 ♗f3 White resigned.

A bit bolder

Fabiano Caruana, who won Wijk aan Zee in 2020, two(!) points ahead of Carlsen, was struggling this time. That, and his natural wish to fight, made the American a perfect opponent for that same Carlsen in the penultimate round. Being due a full point (from Dubov) in the final round, Carlsen knew that a draw was enough for tournament victory. He didn't want to take massive risks, but 'I guess I was feeling a bit bolder than normal'.

NOTES BY
Peter Heine Nielsen

Fabiano Caruana
Magnus Carlsen
Wijk aan Zee 2022 (12)
Sicilian Defence, Rossolimo Attack

1.e4 c5

Perhaps it sounds odd to say that these two players, who played a World Championship match with only draws in the classical part, are an excellent stylistic fit that almost always guarantees an interesting game! Even so, there is some truth in it. Both after their match and during it, their encounters have always been of special interest. In this game, it almost feels as if the World Champion enjoys the prospect of a very aggressive and ambitious opponent and rewards this courage by playing the Sicilian!

In the tournament situation, both players could be reasonably happy with a draw. Magnus would practically clinch first place, while Fabiano Caruana would limit the damage of a tournament gone sour. But both simply seem to enjoy playing each other.

2.♘f3 ♘c6 3.♗b5!?

As in the first part of the 2018 London match, Caruana plays the Rossolimo. The theory has moved on since then though, and the American tries

White's now most fashionable plan.
3...g6 4.0-0 ♗g7 5.c3

5...♘f6
In Norway Chess 2020, Magnus tried 5...e5 and got into trouble. He now sticks to the main line.
6.♖e1 0-0 7.d4 d5 8.e5 ♘e4 9.♗e3

This used to be considered a sub-line in which Black could easily solve his problems, but the emergence of Neural Networks seems to have challenged that opinion. Now it has basically become the main line – a notable difference from the 2018 match.
9...cxd4 10.cxd4 ♕b6

11.♕e2!?

Here 11.♗xc6 is White's surprising main attempt, giving up the bishop pair, but the text has also been played a few times. And it obviously seemed to be part of Caruana's preparation.
11...♗d7 12.♗a4 ♖ac8 13.♘c3 ♘xc3 14.bxc3
A typical strategic motif in this line. White's pawn structure seems weakened with the backward pawn, but that pawn shores up the centre, and Black needs to come up with counterplay before White gets a kingside attack going, often with the typical h4 flank attack.

14...♕d8!
A strong retreat threatening the tactic ...♘xe5, but, more importantly, preparing his next move.
15.♗b3

15...♘a5!
A very important resource. If Black had wasted time defending the d5-pawn with e.g. 15...e6, 16.h4 would have left White strategically winning, with the computer already showing more than +2!
16.♖ac1 ♘xb3!?
A very noteworthy decision. Magnus voluntarily repairs White's broken

pawn structure, knowing that if the play slowed down and White would get to develop his kingside attack, it wouldn't matter anyway, so Black really needs to create counterplay in a hurry.

17.axb3 ♕b6

18.♕a2!?

The computers' preferred move in a strategically highly complex position. 18.♘d2, intending to follow up with 19.h4, would also have made sense. Now, however, Caruana switches his attention to the queenside.

18...a5 19.♕a3 ♖fe8 20.c4 dxc4!?

There were safer options, like 20...a4, but neither player is aiming for simplifications. White now strengthens his central control, with Black hoping to undermine it.

21.bxc4 ♕a6 22.c5 ♗c6 23.♖b1

23...a4!?

The computer gives 23...b5!? 24.cxb6 e6, which is also quite reasonable, but sometimes seems to lead to more exchanges – which, as said, neither player was looking for.

Fabiano Caruana vs. Magnus Carlsen is always a pairing to look forward to. Their clash in Round 12 was another full fight and brought Carlsen tournament victory.

Worth noting is that 23...♗xf3 would have been a blunder, as after 24.gxf3 the damage to White's kingside is slight, since Black has no reasonable way to launch an attack, while still having seriously weakened his queenside (with ...b7), which will soon lack protection.

24.♖ec1

The immediate 24.♘d2 has logic to it, as it forces Black to retreat with 25...♕a8 after 24...♖cd8 25.♖b6, the e2-square is not yet available. Even so, the computer favours White only slightly, since Black is planning ...♕c8, followed by ...f6, with a very unusual and complex position.

24...♖cd8 25.♘d2?!

25...♕e2

It is worth noting that the computer suggests 25...f6!? as possibly the better move, but only because White should now retreat with 26.♘f3!, preventing the black queen from entering the g4-square, and meeting 26...♗xf3 with 27.♖e1!.

26.f3?

A logical move, yet an unusual blunder by Caruana, not only allowing but practically forcing Magnus to play the following exchange sacrifice.

26...♖xd4! 27.♗xd4 ♕xd2 28.♖d1 ♕f4

More than 100 NIC eBooks

Enjoy the advantages of a NIC Interactive eBook on your PC, notebook, smartphone or tablet: it's an exact copy of the printed book, it arrives within a couple of minutes, the postman will not be ringing your doorbell, it doesn't take up space on your bookshelves, and it allows you to replay all the games and variations on the built-in chessboard.

White is nominally ahead in material, but the c6-bishop is solid as a rock, not only pointing at the white kingside but also protecting the passed pawn on a4. In addition, all White's pieces are placed passively and the e5-pawn is inevitably about to fall.

29.♕b4 e6 30.♗c3?

Making things even worse. Keeping the queens on the board would still leave White on the verge of losing after Black ups the pressure with ...h5-h4, which is probably more than the white position can handle. However, the endgame is clinically lost.

30...♕xb4! 31.♗xb4 ♗xe5 32.♗a3 ♗f6 33.♔f2 ♗e7

Carlsen's rating gain from Wijk aan Zee went out of the window again when he drew a game in a Norwegian club match one week later...

According to the traditional way of scoring material White is not doing too badly. Rook vs bishop and two pawns is typically acceptable, but White has no plans whatever and can only passively defend his weakness on c5, while Black gets ready to mobilize his pawn majority.

34.♖b6 ♖c8

Note that ♖xc6 needed to be prevented, but why even bother thinking about it?

35.♖d2 f6 36.f4 e5 37.fxe5 fxe5 38.♖e2 ♖f8+ 39.♔e1 ♖f5 40.♖b1 e4 41.♖c1 ♗h4+!

42.g3 ♗g5 43.♖b1 ♖f3!

Exploiting the weakness created by the bishop check.

44.♗c1 ♗f6 45.♖b6 ♖f5 46.♗a3 ♔f7 47.♖f2 ♖f3!

48.♖xf3

If 48.♗b2, then either ...♗e7, attacking c5, or ...♗d8 win trivially.

48...exf3 49.♔f1 ♗d4

And here Caruana chose to resign. 50.♖b4 ♗e3 was to follow, when White faces an impossible challenge: keep the c5-pawn defended, stop a check on a light square and keep the black king from entering the white camp.

■ ■ ■

Somewhat sad postscript

Thanks to this fifth win (the free point against Dubov obviously not counting) Magnus Carlsen added a grand total of 3.1 points to his rating. More tellingly, he defeated the four other top-10 players in the field, plus the young debutant Praggnanandhaa.

Speaking about his ambition to reach 2900, he explained: 'What I emphasized when I set myself that goal, is that I have to be on top every time I play, to be fully focused and to be always at my best. This, I think, I managed very well here.'

Still, with a gap of some 40 points to close it is not going to be easy. Every little point counts, including the ones you lose, unfortunately. As a sad postscript to a brilliant tournament, Carlsen's rating gain from Wijk aan Zee went out of the window again when he played a game in a Norwegian club match one week later, drawing against 2466-rated Geir Sune Tallaksen Ostmoe, a result that cost the World Champion 4.2 precious rating points... ■

Winning with a dream score

His ambition and plan was to score big (10½ from 13 to be precise) and that's exactly what he did. With his sweeping win in the Challengers, Arjun Erigaisi qualified for next year's Tata Steel top group and earned lavish praise from Magnus Carlsen. Talking to **DIRK JAN TEN GEUZENDAM,** the Indian youngster reflects on his biggest success to date and lays out his plans and hopes for the future.

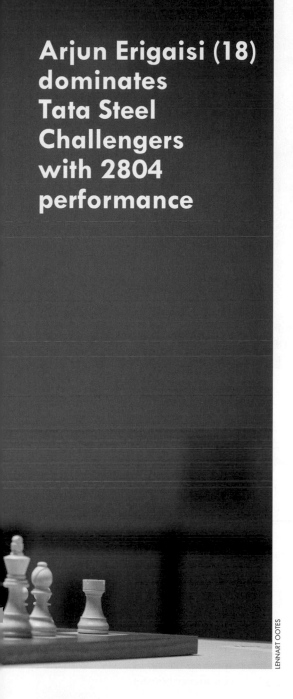

LENNART OOTES

Arjun Erigaisi (18) dominates Tata Steel Challengers with 2804 performance

'**H**e's sensational, he is going to be 2700 very soon. He is by far the best player in the Challengers and he is playing chess in the way that I enjoy. You just can sense that he knows how to play. He has both a good tactical eye and he can switch styles very easily. He's very strong.'

Magnus Carlsen did not mince words when he was asked to comment on the performance of Arjun Erigaisi in the Tata Steel Challengers. For a while already, the World Champion had been acutely aware of the young Indian's talent. If there was one thing that might be called a surprise now, he said, it was Arjun's majestic score in Wijk aan Zee. Winning was one thing, sweeping the field another. Erigaisi finished on 10½ points out of 13 games, a 2804 performance that earned him a spot in next year's Masters. For the statisticians: in this year's Masters only the top three had performances over 2800.

A further quality that must have been to Carlsen's liking was the Indian's stamina and will to win in the final round. His wish to grind, as Carlsen himself likes to grind, when essentially there was no longer anything 'big' at stake for Erigaisi. The previous day he had already clinched first prize when he took an unbridgeable lead of one and a half points over his closest pursuers, Jonas Bjerre of Denmark and Thai Dai Van Nguyen of the Czech Republic.

Yet, in his last game, against French GM Marc Andria Maurizzi, a seemingly unperturbed Arjun set to work with the black pieces – at first without much success. The game began to look drawish, and many believed that he might resign himself to a draw. And why not?

But that's not what he did. With great patience and determination, he kept trying and probing and gradually outplayed Maurizzi, who resigned after 62 moves. It was the last game to finish.

Magnus Carlsen must have nodded in approval. And he was not the only one. Indian GM Surya Ganguly told me what Arjun's last-round effort had reminded him of. And how impressed he had been. 'I remembered the last round of the Tata Steel Masters in 2020. At the start of the round Jeroen (van den Berg, the tournament director) said a few words and congratulated Fabiano Caruana, who one day earlier had won the event with a round to spare. I was playing in the Challengers, and from where I sat I had a direct view of Fabiano. When Jeroen congratulated Fabiano, the spectators gave him a small round of applause. Now, most people would

Magnus Carlsen: 'He has both a good tactical eye and he can switch styles very easily'

acknowledge this and perhaps briefly stand up or at least give a little nod of recognition and gratitude. But Fabiano did nothing, zilch. He didn't even move an eyelid. He kept looking ahead of himself, motionless, and waited for the game to start. And then he set to work and ground down Vladislav Artemiev with the black pieces in 66 moves. Because that was what he had come for. And that's also what Arjun had come for on the final day.'

Motivation

Right after the last game had finished, Arjun's coach Srinath revealed in a tweet that 10½/13 was exactly the goal that his ward had set himself before the tournament. The self-assured revelation, bordering on bragging, seemed to contrast with Arjun's generally quiet and unassuming demeanour, but when we talk on Skype some days later, after his return to India, he assures me that the tweet had been absolutely fine with him. 'No, I didn't mind at all, because after the tournament I realized that it had motivated me. This was the first time

I had set myself such a goal, and I accomplished it. I am very glad I found out that it motivated me, and I will do the same for future events. Or (smilingly) let's say, at least set myself semi-goals.'

It was the first time that Srinath Narayanan, a 28-year-old grandmaster from Chennai, accompanied him to a tournament. 'I have known Srinath since 2018, and it's been more like a mentorship than working together. He advises me on what to do in general, both in chess and also outside of chess. Indian coaches focus on many things and they are very friendly, which makes us feel totally comfortable with them. The relationship between me and Srinath is more like between two friends, rather than a student and a coach. I can discuss anything with him.'

Srinath created a pleasant atmosphere for him in Wijk aan Zee, and so did Surya Ganguly, who joined them for their meals and treated Arjun to stories from his time as Vishy Anand's second. 'There was a great story about Vishy's match against Topalov (in Sofia in 2010). Many flights were cancelled because of the eruption of a volcano in Iceland, and they barely made it to Bulgaria in time by car. Yet Vishy won the match, winning the last game as Black.'

On the free days, they also played games other than chess, mostly Salem and sometimes Avalon. And colleagues might drop by to play, e.g. Sam Shankland and Fabiano Caruana. With a smile Arjun recalls the last day of the tournament. 'An Indian friend from Amsterdam had come over and brought a new game. When I had finally won my last game and returned from the playing hall to the hotel, they were almost done as well.'

Confidence booster

Arjun Erigaisi earned the grandmaster title at the age of 14 years, 11 months and 13 days. He sums up his fast rise almost laconically. 'I started

Arjun Erigaisi and his coach Srinath Narayanan in front of the gallery of winners of the Masters, where he will make his debut next year.

in chess when I was 8 years old. I had tried all kinds of games, like badminton, skating, swimming, but I wasn't connected to those sports. But I was addicted to chess and would spend a lot of nights solving problems; things like that. I was very serious, made all my norms and became a grandmaster. After that I was more or less sure that I would be

'One year ago I used to be scared of a lot of players and I had no faith in my own game'

a professional chess player. I was also managing my studies, data science, but was not too passionate about them. I have decided to give up my studies for now and focus fully on chess.'

Last year, 2021, proved to be a crucial year, with encouraging results that made him grow as a competitive player. 'Let's say, my self-confidence one year ago was nothing

like it is now. I used to be scared of a lot of players and I had no faith in my own game. But I got a lot of opportunities. I won the Indian qualifier for the Champions Chess Tour, and in that leg I became the first Indian to qualify for the knock-out phase. That gave me a lot of confidence. Soon after I did very well in the Lindores Abbey Blitz [shared second with Caruana – DJtG] and then in Kolkata, the Tata Steel India Rapid [which he won one point ahead of Aronian, Praggnanandhaa and Vidit]. And now this. And especially Magnus's words. In general he speaks what he believes, so that's a confidence booster.'

Arjun hails from the state of Telangana in the south-east of India. Telangana formed a state together with Andhra Pradesh until 2014, when there was a split. Andhra Pradesh has quite a lot of chess players, whereas Telangana has 'only' three grandmasters, a modest figure for a country that today boasts an amazing total of 73 grandmasters. On the other hand, most training sessions are held online anyway, as in the morning of our talk, when Arjun joined a session led by Vishy Anand as part of the preparations for the Asian Games.

Slightly over a year ago, Anand's Westbridge Chess Academy also offered him the opportunity to work with Vladimir Kramnik and Boris Gelfand, an experience that he fondly remembers for the insights that they shared.

Likewise, he feels privileged to have the highly experienced Rustam Kasimdzhanov as his main coach. 'When I am at home, we work something like 6 to 8 hours per week. I learned very specific things from Rustam. I soon realized that when I managed to get a position that was close to winning, my technique used to be pretty awful. I lost a lot of advantages, so we worked on that and that made a huge difference. He also showed me a lot of games in which top players finish off very smoothly and many examples of how you can put up more resistance, and not to give up psychologically.'

Clinical

When he mentions the aspects of his play that he has improved thanks to Kasimdzhanov, he seems to explain his choice when he was asked to annotate his favourite games from Wijk aan Zee. He had eight wins to choose from, some of them great fights, but he chose his two most clinical wins.

'Yes, those I see more or less as my best games. There were a few mistakes, but not many, I would say. Especially my game against Zhu Jiner. I played a lot of precise moves, most of them were first choices of the computer, and I blundered only once. I had planned a winning continuation, but the move I played seemed intuitively better, so I went for it.

'If most of my moves match the computer's choice, I am extremely happy with my play. In that game, although I made a blunder, I had made a lot of accurate moves up to that point. And when she blun-

Friends, GMs, rivals and key players in the future of Indian chess: Arjun Erigaisi, Nihal Sarin and Sankalp Gupta.

dered, I had only one winning move, and I found it, so I am happy about it.'

Years ago he tried to emulate the computer by playing against it, but that mainly dented his confidence ('I used to lose like crazy'). Nowadays he uses engines as a tool, when he is working on his openings or reviewing his games.

Arjun is very serious about his chess and works hard, something like eight to ten hours a day, but he tries to be modest about it. He says that Raunak Sadwani, another prodigy (GM, 16 years old) works considerably harder and stresses that he is not so systematic when it comes to working. 'I like working on chess, it's more like something that I find fun to do than that I feel bored that I have to do it.'

Since he wishes to work seriously on chess, his attitude to blitz is ambivalent. Like most youngsters he loves it, and with his good friend Nihal Sarin (GM, 17 years old) he used to play blitz endlessly. But currently he is less interested. 'I don't play as much as I used to. He still does. But we play other games. Do you know Among Us? That's a game where a lot

of people can gather. It's like Salem, but it's online. We need at least four players, and the maximum is fifteen. We're usually around eight players.

'At some point, I was told to play less blitz, but I didn't care much about that and continued. But Srinath turned out to be different and encouraged me to do whatever I like in chess. Now in chess I mostly work on my calculation, openings; things like that.

	Indian top players March 1, 2022	Elo	Born
1	Viswanathan Anand	2751	1969
2	Vidit Gujrathi	2723	1994
3	Pentala Harikrishna	2716	1986
4	Arjun Erigaisi	2660	2003
5	Narayanan.S.L	2658	1998
6	Nihal Sarin	2652	2004
7	Krishnan Sasikiran	2650	1981
8	Adhiban Baskaran	2648	1992
9	Abhijeet Gupta	2628	1989
10	Murali Karthikeyan	2622	1999
11	Rameshbabu Praggnanandhaa	2619	2005
12	S.P. Sethuraman	2619	1993
13	Abhimanyu Puranik	2618	2000
14	Raunak Sadhwani	2616	2005
15	Gukesh D	2614	2006

'I can see a day when we five would make the team and all five of us would be over 2700'

But I still love blitz a lot, like most of my friends. Yes, I also used to play a lot of ultra-bullet. Fifteen seconds per game each. No increments. I remember a day when I played over 800 games of ultra-bullet on Lichess. I played something like five hours. I had a positive score, but I lost rating in the end.'

With 73 grandmasters India has become one of the absolute powerhouses in the chess world. It's an amazing number if we consider that back in 1988, Vishy Anand was India's first-ever grandmaster. Not all of them are active anymore, but competition is inevitably brutal and tough. In that light, it is remarkable how well the very best get along, as Arjun confirms. 'Yes, I am good friends with Nihal (Sarin) and Gukesh, and my best friends are Sankalp Gupta (GM, 18 years old) and Raja Rithvik (GM, 17 years old). Raja Rithvik lives close to me, and Sankalp Gupta lives in another state, but we do meet regularly in tournaments and we share rooms. We usually travel together.'

With his win in Wijk aan Zee, Arjun Erigaisi made a big jump on the rating list. His status has changed and he can cherish hopes for the year ahead and those to come. 'Yes, I am (India's) number four now in the live ratings. I never thought about that. I would be glad if I could make it to the Olympiad team. In a couple of years, we can have a team that can win the Olympiad. Including myself we now have five juniors that are extremely good: Pragg, Nihal, Gukesh, Raunak and myself. I can see a day when we five would make the team and all five of us would be over 2700.'

NOTES BY
Arjun Erigaisi

Arjun Erigaisi
Jonas Buhl Bjerre
Wijk aan Zee 2022 (8)
Sicilian Defence, French Variation

1.e4 c5 2.♘f3 e6
This was a surprising choice of opening, so I decided to counter-surprise him with a calm kingside fianchetto instead of entering main-line theory with 3.d4.
3.g3 ♘c6 4.♗g2 White aims to develop quickly on the kingside instead of going for the central break.

4...d5
With this move, Black decides to accept the IQP [isolated queen pawn – ed.] and try to look for activity.
By far the main move is 4...♘f6, which I was intending to meet with 5.d3 (5.e5 would run into 5...♘g4 6.♕e2 ♕c7, and the pawn on e5 is lost).
A popular line is 5.♕e2 e5. It feels weird for Black to play ...e6 and then ...e5, but Black seems to be doing alright here, as White's queen on e2 is not the best piece in the world.
5.exd5 exd5 6.0-0 ♘f6 7.d4

7...cxd4
7...♗e7 8.dxc5 ♗xc5 (Black has no time for 8...0-0 9.♗e3 ♘g4 10.♗d4, and White holds on to his extra pawn) is another version, which is also fine, but I assume he was unhappy to move the bishop twice. Now, trying to go after Black's uncastled king won't really help White, as the bishop on c5 is staring down the a7-f2 diagonal: 9.♖e1+ ♗e6 10.♘g5?! 0-0 11.♘xe6 fxe6, when 12.♖xe6? fails to 12...♘e4, and White is in big trouble.
8.♘xd4 ♗e7 8...♗g4 only helps White, as the queen would be better placed on d3 and White gains a tempo on h3: 9.♕d3 ♗e7 10.h3 ♗d7 11.♘c3 0-0 12.♗f4.
9.h3
Preventing all kinds of ...♘g4/...♗g4 business before playing ♗e3.
9...0-0 10.♗e3
It is also possible to start with 10.♘c3, but I wanted to keep it flexible, as I had some ♘d2 ideas in mind.

10...♘xd4?!
Clearly, 10...♖e8 should have been played. Releasing the tension was not the best idea, but his whole point of 10...♘xd4 was based on 13...♗b4, which turns out to be a blunder.
11.♗xd4 ♗f5 Now ...♕c8, with a double attack on h3 and c2, is the threat.
12.♘c3 This is already a slight edge for White, as the bishop on d4 looks like a monster.
12...♘e4 13.♖e1
Unfortunately for him, he now picked up the bishop, intending to go 13...♗b4, only to realize that this would run into 14.♗xg7.

13...♗f6 This was the best move available for him after he had touched the bishop, but this is already close to lost, as Black is losing a pawn by force. It was psychologically very tough for him to continue and offer the best resistance, after ending up in such a horrendous position in just 13 moves! But if he had not touched the bishop, his game would not have been easy either: 13...♖e8 14.♕d3, and White retains a solid advantage, as Black's set-up is not harmonious.

Or 13...♘xc3 14.♗xc3 ♗e6 15.♗d4 ♗f6 16.c3, and White has an excellent advantage, as his light-squared bishop spits fire on the poor d5-pawn.

14.♗xf6 ♘xf6 15.♘xd5 ♘xd5 16.♕xd5

16...♕xd5 16...♗xc2 was another variation that I considered during the game, but keeping the queens on only helps White, as his queen will be superior to Black's after 17.♕xb7.

17.♗xd5 ♗xc2

Taking the h3-pawn – 17...♗xh3 – is a bad idea, since 18.♗xb7 ♖ab8 19.♖e7 would give me a clear two-pawn majority on the queenside, and my pawns would soon start marching down the board.

18.♖e7 18.♗xb7 was also possible, but that pawn is mine in any case.

18...♖ad8 I had been expecting 18...♗f5, and now 19.♗xb7 ♖ab8 20.b4! ♗xh3 21.b5, and although the material is equal, White's activity and the outside passer on the queenside give him a large advantage.

19.♗xb7 White's aim is to win the a7-pawn and create outside passers on the queenside.

19...a5 Black intends to get the pawn to a4 and restrict White's b2-pawn.

In case of 19...♗f5, White continues 20.♗g2.

20.♖ae1 In view of Black's plan, 20.b3! would have been a good move here: 20...a4 21.b4.

20...a4 A critical line was 20...♗f5, as Black would have good drawing chances if he managed to bring the bishop to e6: 21.♖7e5 ♗e6 (21...♗xh3 22.♖xa5, and the queenside pawns win easily) 22.b3! ♖d7 23.♗f3 a4 24.bxa4 ♗xa2 25.a5.

ANALYSIS DIAGRAM

The whole point now is that, unlike in the 22.♖xa5 line, White's rook is not blocking his own pawn. This is winning, but some technique is still required.

21.♗c6!

Putting pressure on the target.

21...♖d4 22.♖d7

Trying to trade off Black's active rook, after which the pawn on a4 would be extremely weak.

22...♖b4 23.♖d2

23...♗f5

As 23...♖xb2 runs into 24.♗e4, and Black is lost.

23...♖c4 would be followed by 24.♗d5 ♖cc8 25.♖c1 (true to the spirit of the position – trading off Black's active rook) 25...♗f5 26.♖xc8 ♖xc8 27.♗c6 a3 28.b4, and White is on the verge on winning.

24.a3

24.♔g2 takes a different approach, keeping the h3-pawn alive and playing it slow, which is perfectly sensible too.

24...♖b6 25.♗xa4 ♗xh3

White has finally achieved what he wanted – two passed queenside

pawns – and now it's just a matter of technique.

26.♖e5

26.♖e3 was the most precise: 26...♗e6 27.b4.

26.♖e8 would have been the simplest, if not for 26...♖xe8 27.♗xe8 ♔f8 28.♗a4 ♗g4, after which White's bishop is stranded and it's tough to roll the pawns, although this still should be won with some struggle. White should not rush with 26.b4?, as after 26...♖a6 White would lose the a3-pawn.

26...♖fb8?!

This doesn't change the result of the game, but it is a dubious move because it makes White's job easier. 26...g6 would have offered more resistance, as 27.♖b5 can now be met by 27...♖a6.

27.♖b5! ♔f8 28.♖d8+

28.♖xb6 also wins: 28...♖xb6 29.♗d1 ♔e7 30.b4 ♗d7 31.f4.

28...♖xd8 29.♖xb6

29...♗e6

He could have tried to offer better resistance with 29...g5.

30.♗b3

And Black resigned.

NOTES BY
Arjun Erigaisi

Zhu Jiner
Arjun Erigaisi
Wijk aan Zee 2022 (9)
Ruy Lopez, Morphy Defence

1.e4 e5 2.♘f3 ♘c6 3.♗b5 a6 4.♗a4 ♗c5

An old move that is being tried out in these modern days, although not as frequently as the main Ruy Lopez, in which the knight goes to f6. In this variation, Black intends to put his knight on e7.

5.c3 The most challenging reaction, intending an immediate strike in the centre.

After 5.0-0, 5...d6 is important (as 5...♘ge7 would run into 6.♘xe5 ♘xe5 7.d4, with a white edge), when play continues 6.c3 ♗a7.

5...♘ge7 6.d4 exd4 7.cxd4

7...♗b4+

The whole point. But for this move, Black would be close to losing already, as White would take control of the centre after 7...♗a7 8.d5.

8.♗d2 ♗xd2+ 9.♕xd2

9.♘bxd2 is safer, but also less ambitious, with Black also continuing 9...d5.

9...d5 10.exd5 ♕xd5

10...♘xd5 is less risky, but also leaves Black with fewer prospects.

11.♘c3 11.0-0 is a safer line, when White retains a slight edge after 11...0-0 12.♘c3.

11...♕e6+

12.♔f1

The most natural move, with the rook swinging over to the e-file and the isolated pawn forking on d5. At first sight, it looks as if Black's coordination is not great, but there is a wonderful resource.

This means that 12.♕e3 was called for to ensure that White remains on top in the endgame.

12...♕c4+ 13.♔g1

13...♗e6!

The check followed by this move doesn't look natural at all, since it looks as if the queen is getting trapped on c4 – but magically nothing is working for White.

14.♘e5

14.a3 wouldn't work, due to 14...0-0-0 15.b3 ♘xd4! (the whole point)

Zhu Jiner, the number one junior in the world on the girls' list, was clearly delighted to play in Wijk aan Zee.

16.bxc4 ♘xf3+ 17.gxf3 ♖xd2, and Black is winning.

And after 14.b3 Black has 14...♕b4, and the queen escapes.

14...♕b4

15.a3 Practically speaking a slightly dubious move, I think, since White doesn't get any structural advantage in return for wasting some tempi with her king.

15.♘xc6 ♘xc6 16.♗xc6+ bxc6 17.♖d1 would lead to a double-edged game.

15...♕b6 16.♗xc6+ ♘xc6 17.♘xc6 ♕xc6!

This is a very smart move.

18.h4?

This is certainly a bad move, since Black now gets a dream position in which he is more active and White has a weak isolated d-pawn.

This is why 18.d5 0-0-0 19.♖d1 was called for (due to his activity, Black is far better in the endgame after 19.dxc6 ♖xd2), exchanging the queens and liquidating to an endgame that's very close to equal.

18...0-0-0 19.h5

White tries to breathe life into her rook from h4. I really love the way I dealt with this.

19...♗d5

Hitting the g2-pawn.

20.f3

20.♘xd5 ♖xd5 21.♖h4 ♖hd8 is better for Black, since there is a lot of pressure on the d4- and h5-pawns.

20...♕f6

Preventing the rook from coming to h4.

21.♕f2 ♗b3

Hitting the d4-pawn.

22.♖h4

And it looks as if White has achieved what she intended, doesn't it?

22...♖he8

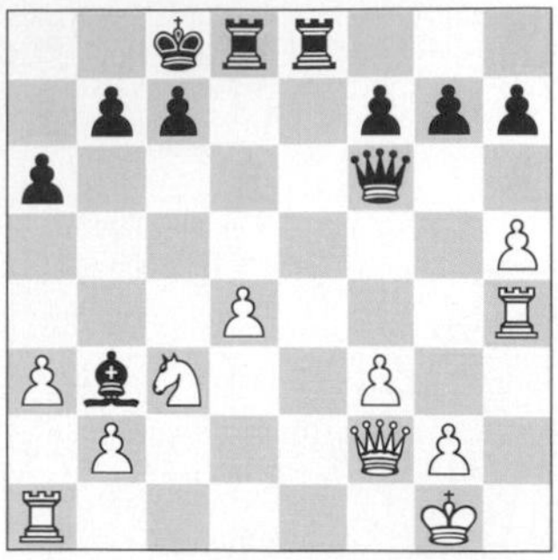

Yes, the rook is active now, which is pretty much what White wanted, but now the problem for White is the poor coordination of her pieces. The queen is paralyzed on f2, since it has to protect h4 and d4, the rook on a1 struggles to find a good square, the knight on c3 cannot move, and the rook on h4 can move but can't really help White. Black's pieces, on the other hand, are all very active.

23.♖g4 ♕h6 Giving way for the f7-pawn while hitting the pawn on h5.

24.♖e1 f5 25.♖h4

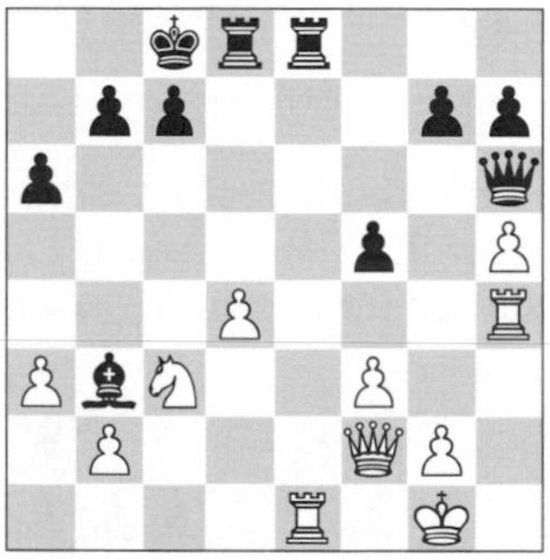

25...♗f7 Black is far better, but 25...♖xe1+ 26.♕xe1 ♕f6 27.♕f2 ♗f7 was still stronger – it would have been more accurate to paralyze White's major pieces completely and only then return with the bishop to put pressure on the h5-pawn.

26.♔h2 26.♖xe8 ♖xe8 would be very good for Black.

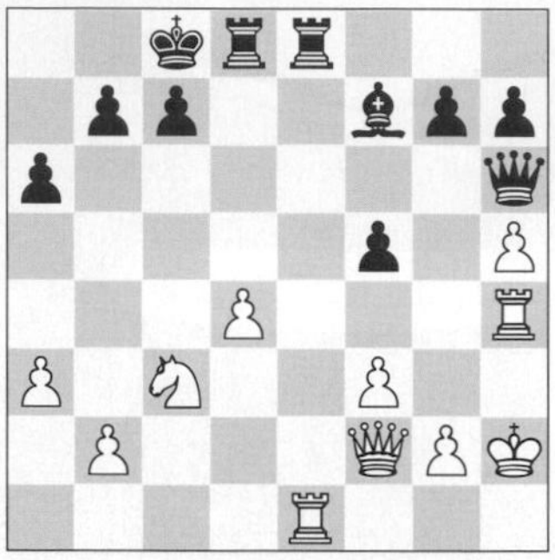

26...♗xh5 Grabbing the pawn! A good alternative was 26...♖xe1 27.♕xe1 ♗xh5 28.♕e5 ♕g5 29.♖h3 ♖e8, also with a clear advantage for Black.

27.♖xe8 ♖xe8 28.♕g3 Because 28.g4 will fail to win the bishop, since Black has a check along the h2-b8 diagonal: 28...fxg4 29.fxg4 ♕d6+, and White is lost,

28...♕g6 When you're up material, trade pieces!

29.♕f4 ♕f7

Consolidating the extra pawn by stabilizing everything.

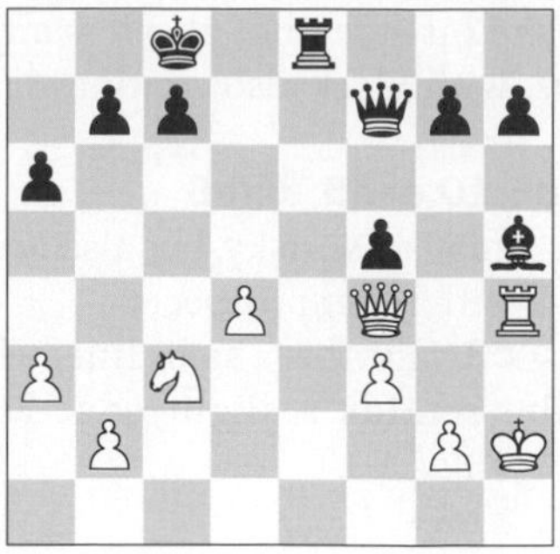

30.d5 ♗g6 31.d6

White finally gets rid of the weak d-pawn, but it's too late; the damage has been done.

31...♖d8

Liquidating to an endgame.

32.dxc7 ♕xc7 33.♕xc7+ ♔xc7

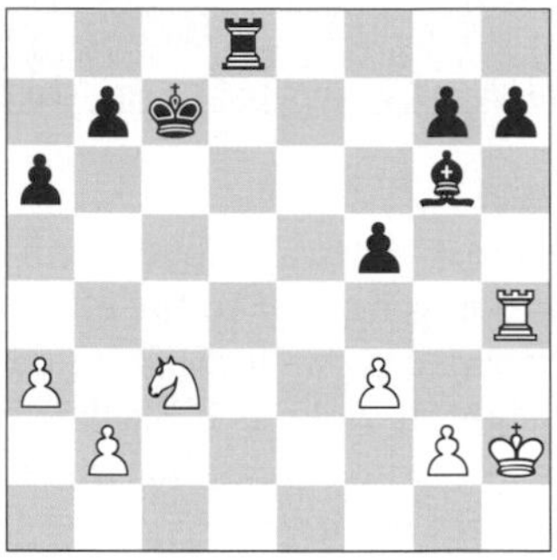

34.♘e2

Not a blunder, White tries to do something concrete which is sensible. After 34.♖c4+ ♔b8 it is just an extra pawn for Black.

34...♖d2

Also strong was 34...h6 35.♖c4+ ♔b8 36.♖d4 ♔c7.

35.♘f4 ♖xb2

An interesting alternative was 35...♔b6!? 36.♘xg6 hxg6 37.♖h7 ♖d7, with a large advantage for Black.

36.♘xg6 hxg6 37.♖h7

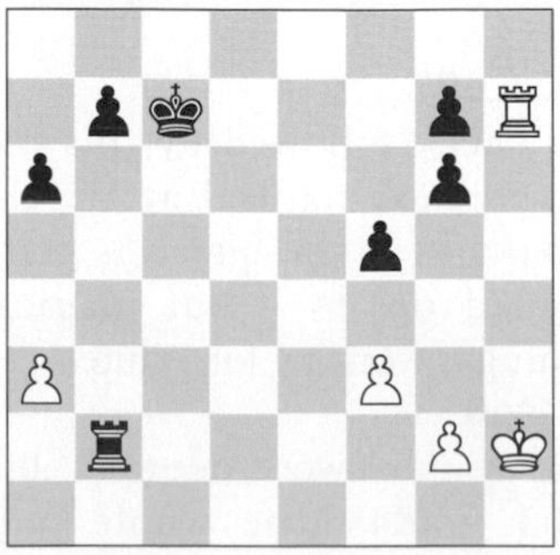

Wijk aan Zee 2022 Challengers

					1	2	3	4	5	6	7	8	9	10	11	12	13	14		TPR
1	Arjun Erigaisi	IGM	IND	2632	*	½	1	½	½	½	1	1	1	1	1	½	1	1	10½	2806
2	Thai Dai Van Nguyen	IGM	CZE	2613	½	*	1	½	½	½	½	½	½	½	1	½	1	1	8½	2667
3	Jonas Buhl Bjerre	IGM	DEN	2586	0	0	*	1	1	½	1	½	1	½	1	½	1	½	8½	2669
4	Rinat Jumabayev	IGM	KAZ	2631	½	½	0	*	0	1	½	½	1	1	½	1	½	½	7½	2612
5	Erwin l'Ami	IGM	NED	2622	½	½	0	1	*	0	½	½	1	½	½	1	½	1	7½	2613
6	Lucas van Foreest	IGM	NED	2539	½	½	½	0	1	*	½	½	½	1	0	1	½	½	7	2591
7	Volodar Murzin	IM	RUS	2519	0	½	0	½	½	½	*	½	½	1	½	1	½	1	7	2593
8	Max Warmerdam	IGM	NED	2607	0	½	½	½	½	½	½	*	½	0	½	1	½	1	6½	2557
9	Surya Shekhar Ganguly	IGM	IND	2627	0	½	0	0	0	½	½	½	*	½	1	½	1	1	6	2527
10	Daniel Dardha	IGM	BEL	2532	0	½	½	0	½	0	0	1	½	*	0	1	½	1	5½	2506
11	Marc'Andria Maurizzi	IGM	FRA	2502	0	0	0	½	½	1	½	½	0	1	*	0	½	0	4½	2455
12	Polina Shuvalova	IM	RUS	2516	½	½	½	0	0	0	0	0	½	0	1	*	½	1	4½	2454
13	Roven Vogel	IM	GER	2452	0	0	0	½	½	½	½	½	0	½	½	½	*	0	4	2428
14	Jiner Zhu	WGM	CHN	2478	0	0	½	½	0	½	0	0	0	0	1	0	1	*	3½	2392

That was the whole point.

37...♔b6?

I was lured into doing this, as intuitively it seemed winning with Black's king more active.

After 37...♖b6 38.♖xg7+ ♔b8 Black keeps the extra queenside pawn, and with some difficulty this can be converted into a win: 39.♔g3 a5 40.♔f4 a4, and White is lost.

38.♖xg7 ♔a5 39.♖xg6 ♔a4

40.♖g5?

This loses because of my reply. The only move that would have held was 40.♖f6!, the point being that after 40...♖b5 41.g4 fxg4 42.fxg4 ♔xa3 43.♔g3.

ANALYSIS DIAGRAM

White seems to be holding, since Black's rook is in the way of his own pawns, whereas White's pawn has no obstacles to navigate through.

After 40...♔xa3 41.♖xf5 b5 42.♔h3 White would hold, because Black cannot rush with his b-pawn, as this would run into ♖a5+, and after 42...a5 43.g4 a4 44.g5 White is in time to march his g-pawn: 44...b4 45.g6 ♖b1 46.♔g2 ♖b2+ 47.♔h3 ♖b1, with a draw by repetition.

With eight wins and zero losses, Arjun Erigaisi finished two points ahead of his closest pursuers and way ahead of the rest.

40...f4!! As after 40...♖b5 41.g4 ♖b2+ (41...fxg4 ends in a forced draw after 42.♖xb5 axb5 43.fxg4 ♔xa3 44.g5 b4 45.g6 b3 46.g7 b2 47.g8♕ b1♕ 48.♕a8+ ♔b2 49.♕xb7+) 42.♔g3 fxg4 43.f4,

ANALYSIS DIAGRAM

Black's rook gets in the way of his own pawns, just like before, and it becomes

a matter of quality over quantity! White's single pawn marches forward very quickly, which is enough to hold the game to a draw.

41.♖f5 ♔xa3 42.♖xf4 b5

The difference between this and the other line in which White's rook was on f5 is that Black can rush forward with his b-pawn now.

43.♔h3 43.♖f5 falls one tempo short: 43...a5 44.♔h3 a4 45.g4 b4 46.g5 ♖c2 47.g6 ♖c8, and Black wins.

43...b4 44.g4 b3 45.♖f5

Or 45.g5 ♖b1 46.♖f6 a5 47.♖b6 b2 48.f4 ♖f1, and wins.

45...♖a2! Another important move! Ensuring that the a-pawn stays alive.

46.g5 46.♖a5+ ♔b4.

46...b2 47.♖f6

47...a5

No rush! 47...b1♕?? would have been a terrible blunder: 48.♖xa6+ ♚b3 49.♖b6+ ♚c2 50.♖xb1 ♚xb1 51.♚g4, and White can make a draw.

48.♖b6 ♖a1 49.f4 b1♕ 50.♖xb1 ♖xb1 51.g6 ♖g1 52.f5 ♖g5

White resigned here in view of 53.♚h4 ♖xf5 54.g7 ♖f1! 55.g8♕ ♖h1+ 56.♚g5 ♖g1+ 57.♚f6 ♖xg8.

And then there was this...

With his superb play and unchallenged victory, Arjun Erigaisi easily attracted most of the attention, but he was not the only one in the Tata Steel Challengers that entertained the online audience. And the colleagues in the Masters for that matter.

When he was interviewed about the Indian rising star, Magnus Carlsen did not have to think long when he was asked to name his favourite game from the Challengers. 'Obviously, Arjun played some nice games, but I am going with a bit of a Scandinavian flavour. I must say that I enjoyed Jonas Bjerre's game against Ganguly. That was nice.' We could not agree more.

NOTES BY
Jonas Bjerre

**Jonas Buhl Bjerre
Surya Shekhar Ganguly**
Wijk aan Zee 2022 (9)
Queen's Gambit Declined, Semi-Tarrasch

1.d4 ♘f6 2.c4 e6 3.♘f3 d5 4.♘c3
This was my first time to play this move.

4...c5 5.e3 ♘c6 6.a3 dxc4 7.♗xc4 a6 8.0-0 b5 9.♗a2 ♗b7 10.♕e2 cxd4 11.♖d1 b4 12.exd4 bxc3 13.d5 ♘xd5 14.♖xd5 ♕c7 15.♖d3 ♗e7 16.♖xc3 0-0

17.♘g5!?
As I recalled the line during the game, Black should first kick the rook off the third rank with 16...♗f6, and only then castle. I was wrong, but anyway my attempt to use the rook in the attack wasn't without danger for Black.

17.♗e3 was Dubov's choice against Vidit in the Grand Prix in Berlin, shortly after Wijk aan Zee – a calmer and probably more sensible approach. White had some pressure, but in the end it was a draw.

17...h6?
After a long think my opponent decides to check my hand.

The most obvious alternative was 17...♗f6 18.♖h3. I think we both missed 18...♕e5!, which forces the queens off the board and leaves Black without any issues, since I wouldn't have the time to capture the h7-pawn. After 19.♕e4 ♕xe4 20.♘xe4 the game is equal.

I was calculating 18...h6, which once again dares me to sacrifice the knight, but after 19.♘xe6 Black unfortunately has 19...♖ae8!, which also forces the queen swap: 20.♘xc7 ♖xe2 21.♔f1 ♖c2.

18.♘xf7
18.♘xe6? is refuted by 18...fxe6 19.♕xe6+ ♚h8 20.♗xh6 ♖f6! (otherwise ♘xe6 would be crushing) 21.♗xg7+ ♚xg7 22.♖g3+

ANALYSIS DIAGRAM

22...♕xg3!, and Black wins.

18...♖xf7 19.♕xe6 ♖af8

20.♗xh6!
The main point behind ♘g5. Black's king is now seriously weakened and has no place to hide from my sniper on a2.

20...♗f6!

The only defence. Ganguly told me after the game that he thought he had seen this position before.

After 20...♕d6 the endgame would be hopeless against so many pawns: 21.♕xd6 ♗xd6 22.♖d3, and White is winning.

This was a critical moment, when I had to choose a direction for the next phase.

21.♖c2

Finally I pulled back to preserve the pressure.

21.♖c5 looks more active than having the rook on c2, but I decided against it to avoid exchanging queens: 21...♕e7 22.♗e3 ♕xe6 23.♗xe6 ♔h7 24.♗xf7 ♖xf7. Now b2 is under fire

and pinned, plus Black's pieces are better placed than in the previous endgame, which I thought would give drawing chances.

But first of all I should refrain from following my first instinct of deploying the rook in my attack with 21.♖g3?, due to a little trap: 21...♘d4 22.♕xf6? ♘e2+ 23.♔h1 ♘xg3+ (check!) 24.hxg3 gxf6, and White can resign.

21...♔h7

21...♔h8? was more desirable, to avoid a later check, but it would run into 22.♕h3! ♗c8 23.♕h5, and White wins.

22.♗e3

After 22.♕f5+ ♔xh6! (after 22...g6, 23.♕h3 wins, as 23...♗c8 can be

met by 24.g4!), I was unfortunately unable to find anything, despite the black king's adventurous route to g5. After 23.♕h3+ ♔g5! Black is up a lot of material, but 24.g3 makes the position seem highly unclear. Maybe White is better after some long engine lines, but for a practical game there was no reason to play like this.

22...♕d7 23.♕e4+ g6

24.♗xf7?!

It was a bit too early to cash in, as the attack fades away with the disappearance of this bishop.

The immediate 24.♖d2 was stronger: 24...♘e5 (24...♘d4 loses to 25.♕f4, as ♕h6+ is a devastating threat)

25.♖xd7 ♗xe4 26.♖d4!, and White wins back adequate material.

24...♖xf7 25.♖d2 ♘d4!

I thought this move wasn't possible here either, but the complications now actually work out in Black's favour.

26.♕f4 ♕c6 27.f3 g5!

An unpleasant surprise. If Black is not aggressive, the white pawn army would probably prevail.

28.♕g3

The obvious retreat 28.♕g4? would be met by 28...♘b3!, and although Black's king looks exposed, there are not enough pieces left to exploit this.

28...♘f5

Creating counterplay. All the previous excitement had brought us both down quite low on the clock. With a still super-unbalanced position, it was difficult to stay in control.

29.♕f2 ♔g6 30.♖ad1 ♕c7 31.♖c2 ♕b8 32.h3!

Not entirely calculated, but it turns out to be very clever. ...♗e5 looks scary, but the threats are, in fact, limited.

Just like last year, Wijk aan Zee felt eerily deserted without the hundreds of amateur players and visitors that normally flock to the Dutch coastal village.

32...♗e5 33.♗a7 ♗h2+?

It was difficult to realize that moving the queen was called for.

34.♔h1 ♕f4 35.♕b6+ ♔g7

Down to our last minutes, we both lost track entirely.

36.♕e6?

36.♕d8! prepares the same idea of ♖d7, but also stops ...♗xf3 by protecting the d1-rook.

36...♗g3?

Played with just a couple of seconds left! It was a bit of a panic move. Neither of us managed to make 36...♗xf3! work, but after 37.gxf3 ♕xf3+ 38.♖g2, 38...f4! seals the line. I have no threats and a perpetual will follow, either after 39.♖d7 ♘g3+ 40.♔h2 ♘e4+ or after 39.♗d4+ ♘xd4 40.♖xd4 ♕f1+ 41.♖g1 ♕f3+.

37.♖d7 ♘d6

38.♗b8? This wins, but 38.♖cc7! is mate in 12! Some kind of psychological block stopped me from playing this, as I feared for my back rank in the time-pressure.

38...♕a4!

This almost gave me a heart attack. Both my rooks are under attack, and my first rank looks very vulnerable.

39.♗xd6 I found a line with no risk at all and good winning chances after move 40 – I thought. However, 39.♖dc7! covers everything after 39...♛d4 40.♖c1. Here I keep a big advantage and Black is the one having to figure out how not to lose quickly.

39...♖xd7 40.♗xg3 ♖d1+ 41.♔h2 ♛xc2

With an extra 50 minutes on the clock and the smoke having cleared, it was frustrating to realize that I had let the win slip.

42.♛e7+ ♔g6 43.♛xb7

43...♛b1? The precise square was 43...♛c1!, and now:

– 44.♛e4+ 44...♔f7 45.♗e5 (this was my idea) 45...♖h1+ 46.♔g3 ♛e1+!, and Black can steer the endgame to a draw. With three pawns for the exchange, the pawns are still too difficult to advance.

– 44.♛xa6+ ♔h5 45.♗e1. Now Black has a check: 45...♛c7+! (and not 45...♛f4+? 46.g3 or 45...♖xe1 46.g4+ ♔h4 47.♛h6 mate).

44.♛xa6+ ♔h5

45.♗e1! A nice study-like finish exploiting the precarious position of the black king. It took me a couple of attempts to calculate all the final traps.

45...♛xb2 46.♛e6 ♛b8+

47.♔g1! 47.♔h1 ♛g3, and Black draws. **47...♛a7+** 47...♛g3 48.♔f1!, and Black is short of moves and loses.

48.♔f1 The checks are over, and so is the game. 48.♔h1? would let Black escape with a draw after 48...♛f2!.

48...♖xe1+ 49.♛xe1 ♛xa3 50.♛e5

This endgame is easily winning.

50...♛a6+ 51.♔g1 ♔h6 52.♔h2 ♛b6 53.♔g3 ♛a6 54.♔g4 ♛c8+ 55.♔g3 ♛a6 56.h4 gxh4+ 57.♔xh4 ♛b6 58.f4 ♔h7 59.f5 ♛h6+ 60.♔g4 ♛d2 61.♛e7+ Black resigned. ■

COLOPHON

PUBLISHER: Remmelt Otten
EDITOR-IN-CHIEF:
Dirk Jan ten Geuzendam
HONORARY EDITOR: Jan Timman
CONTRIBUTING EDITOR: Anish Giri
EDITORS: Peter Boel, René Olthof
PRODUCTION: Joop de Groot
TRANSLATOR: Piet Verhagen
SALES AND ADVERTISING: Edwin van Haastert
PHOTOS AND ILLUSTRATIONS IN THIS ISSUE:
Pierre Adenis/World Chess, Chess-Content Production,
Jurriaan Hoefsmit, Lennart Ootes, Gabor Papp,
Russian Chess Federation/Chess Museum, Russian State
Archive of Film and Photo Documents, Berend Vonk
COVER PHOTO: Pierre Adenis/World Chess
COVER DESIGN: Hélène Bergmans

© No part of this magazine may be reproduced,
stored in a retrieval system or transmitted in any
form or by any means, recording or otherwise,
without the prior permission of the publisher.

NEW IN CHESS
P.O. BOX 1093
1810 KB ALKMAAR
THE NETHERLANDS

PHONE: 00-31-(0)72-51 27 137
SUBSCRIPTIONS: nic@newinchess.com
EDITORS: editors@newinchess.com

WWW.NEWINCHESS.COM

MY 60 MEMORABLE LOSSES

Or... why you should write your first chess book

'Then I threw all my pieces on the floor and left the room.' I was telling my daughter Josie about being a sore loser.

She laughed. 'How old were you? Like, around six or seven?' She asked a reasonable question. She's a reasonable person.

I was 18 years old.

I didn't go to school for a week after that. I had been playing for my school's high school team. I was already the high school champion of my state so I thought that made me a 2800+ player.

As I was leaving the playing room that day (the gym) even my own teammates were laughing at me. Nobody wanted me to win. Because...I don't know. That's just the way people are. Not every action has a motive. Not every motive has a reason.

I'd like to think I'm not a sore loser anymore. But I am. It just has a different flavour. Like Strawberry vs Vanilla.

After a 25-year-break from tournaments I decided to reclaim my full mastery of chess and play in a tournament again. I played in the Washington Chess Congress in DC in the US last October. And as the kids say on the Internet...'and you wouldn't believe what happened next...' Except you would.

I had 5 LOSSES and 3 draws! I was very upset with myself. What the hell is going on? What the hell? I couldn't sleep. No wins? Five losses? This wasn't like it was 25 years ago. I called my wife. 'Am I sick?' I asked her. 'Maybe a brain tumour?'

I kept going in the tournament. I didn't want to give up. And I did try to re-frame it. 'This will be a treasure trove of games to study so I can improve.' Which is true.

Yes, you can learn from all of your games – wins and losses. And yes, it's a cliché to say you only learn from losses. Or, in the case of normal adult life, you only learn from your hard times.

But the cliché is mostly true. When I win, it's because my true genius FINALLY reveals itself. 'This will be a game I make a video about and people will learn from it for centuries,' I will be thinking as I deliver the winning blow. 'This is the perfect game. Like a computer played it.' Etc.

But when I lose, something went terribly, terribly wrong. Something awful happened. I didn't sleep the night before. Or my opponent is cheating. Or aliens invaded. Something.

At the very least, I feel regret.

I used to say, 'I have no regrets. If I didn't go broke, lose my house, lose everything, I wouldn't be the man I am today.'

But I do regret. All the time. And when I lose a game, I regret everything. The choice of opening. The missed tactic. Rejecting the draw offer when I was winning.

In a famous study of Olympic medallists, they showed people the faces of all the Olympians at the moment they were awarded their medals on the podium.

They showed closeups of the faces at the moments the medals were announced. They asked the participants in the study which faces seemed the happiest.

Of course, the gold medallists were the happiest. But the interesting thing is, the bronze medallists were also ranked very happy (the visual cue is that when people have what is called a 'Duchenne smile' the smile is more genuine. A smile where the eyes are smiling as well).

The silver medallists were miserable.

That's the difference between 'If only...' and 'At least...'.

If only I had seen that winning tactic.

As opposed to: at least I found that stalemate and drew the game.

If only I had prepared harder.

At least I had a fun time and learned something.

'If only...' people improve in whatever domain they feel regret in. The 'at least' people were happy in the short term but were not as motivated to learn

However, many studies since then have shown that the 'If only...' people improve in whatever domain they feel regret in. The 'at least' people were happy in the short term but were not as motivated to learn.

Regret is a motivator.

'If only I had not missed that tactic...' means that before the next tournament you study 1000 tactics. 'If only I had studied that line of the Sämisch...' means I go home, open up Chessable (thank you Gawain Jones for your lifetime repertoire KID), and study the Sämisch with '7.d5'.

Regret is my guide on the map of my failures. It's my way out into the promised land. It's Will Smith in The Legend of Bagger Vance or Yoda in Return of the Jedi or Botvinnik in Kasparov-Karpov 1984.

There are three ways to cope with regret according to Dan Pink in his book *The Power of Regret*.

Disclose. Break out those losses, examine every move, determine the moves or actions even prior to the game that you regret the most.

Reframe: The past is the past. But studying these games and moves and actions will make you better in the future.

Extract a lesson: Study that course, study those tactics, figure out how to sleep better in the middle of tournaments, get a coach to go through the game with you (Thank you, Jesse Kraai, for forcing me to write ten+ pages of notes on each game).

This is all great and will make one improve (or, perhaps, even enjoy more the games that were so disappointing. After all, chess is a game we all love so let's try to enjoy every minute of it – on the board and off).

But there's one thing further I am going to do and I think you should do also.

My 60 Memorable Losses

Ten years ago I had already written five or six books with mainstream publishers. The prior two had not sold so well. Which means I was dead to publishers at that moment. Nobody would give me a book deal.

And self-publishing had a huge stigma attached to it. 'What, nobody likes your book so you called up a printer and published it yourself?' People would laugh.

But Amazon changed the game. You could just upload a book and publish it and people had no idea (or didn't care) who the publisher was. If people liked the book, it sold. If they didn't, it wouldn't.

I hired an editor, a cover designer, an interior designer, and I wrote a book and made it look like any other professionally published book. I wouldn't let anyone else choose me. Who are they? What do they know about publishing that I don't?

I wrote my book, got a great cover, etc. and did a whole marketing campaign. When the book was all finished I didn't have to call a vanity publisher and print up 58 copies. Those days of stigma or over.

I uploaded it to Amazon, listed it as a kindle and a paperback (they print on demand) and even did the audio version of the book.

The book, *Choose Yourself!*, was published in June, 2013 and sold over a million copies. I still get a nice check every month from Amazon.

There are three ways to cope with regret according to Dan Pink in his book *The Power of Regret*

Now every publisher wants me to publish a book with them and sometimes I do. But my self-published books are by far the books that sell the best. I've written 24 books now.

The most famous chess book, *My 60 Memorable Games*, is by Bobby Fischer. Many people have since copied the style. For instance, I highly recommend Andy Soltis' book, *Magnus Carlsen: 60 Memorable Games*.

But what's to stop me from writing, *My 60 Memorable Losses*.

What?? How could I do that? I'm not a world champion! Or a grandmaster! Who would care about my games, let alone my losses?

Maybe nobody. There are many reasons to self-publish:

A) To sell a lot of books and make money without the bureaucracy of mainstream publishing putting their foot on your neck while you squirm on the ground.

One study shows that self-published books, on average, rank higher on Amazon than mainstream published books. Meaning: the average self-published book sells better. Examples: *The Martian* and *50 Shades of Grey* were originally self-published and then republished later when publishers saw how well they were doing.

Mainstream publishers contacted me and wanted to republish *Choose Yourself* but I would say, 'no'. I had chosen myself!

B) To be able to say, 'I've published a book.' It's a dream for many to write and publish a book. If two people are up for a job and they have the same qualifications but one published a book and the other didn't, the one who published the book will get the job.

C) For your great-great-great grandchildren. Let them know who you are. So what if only seven people read the memoir of your fascinating life. Those seven people will be the great-great grandkids who wish they had known you. Now they get to.

Self-publishing a book is a gift to your descendants. I wish I could read something written by my great-great-grandparents.

D) Because it holds you accountable. You won't just study a loss for five minutes with a computer. You will really learn from those games.

I'm going to write *My 60 (or 20, or 10) Memorable Losses* because it will hold me accountable to really studying these losses, identifying my mistakes, extracting the lesson (as recommended in *The Power of Regret*).

I'm going to write *My 60 (or 20, or 10) Memorable Losses* because it will hold me accountable to really studying these losses, identifying my mistakes, extracting the lesson

And because I am going to write it, design it, upload it to Amazon, publish it for the world to see, I better learn what I can, study what I can, show every lesson, every nuance of the game I missed. And it will satisfy another dream of mine: writing a chess book. Who can stop me?

In other words: I will learn from my mistakes, appreciate the nuances of the game, enjoy the value of writing a book, improve as a chess player, improve as a writer, even improve as a businessman (I will market the book if I think it's good), and my descendants who play chess can see what an idiot I was.

Who cares if people snicker and say, 'He's not even World Champion. Who cares about his '50 memorable losses'.'

I care. And, if you write such a book – which I hope you do – maybe you will care also.

Viswanathan Anand's most memorable loss

This weekend I am playing in the 'Georgia State Senior Championship'. You have to be over 50 years old to play (no kids!). The winner gets to play in the US Senior Championship.

GM Alonso Zapata won the last time this tournament was held so I looked at his games. Maybe I will play him tomorrow!

Amazingly, in 1988 he had a six-move win against future World Champion Viswanathan Anand:
1.e4 e5 2.♘f3 ♘f6 3.♘xe5 d6 4.♘f3 ♘xe4 5.♘c3 ♗f5

And now after the next white move, Anand resigned. So White to move and win.

There's not many nuances to this game of course. And I'm not sure how motivating this game was. And why did even Anand miss this?

Interestingly, Tony Miles vs Larry Christiansen reached the same position a year earlier and White did NOT make the winning sixth move and the game ended in a draw.

I'm sure people laughed at Anand afterwards. Maybe he even cried himself to sleep that night. I certainly would have.

Anand has played this variation 70 times since in tournament games. He's won 40 and lost 10 and drew the rest for a win rate of 80% in the definitive games. Compare this to his overall win rate of 60% and you can be the judge: did this loss motivate Anand more than his usual game?

Would he include this game in his perhaps future book *My 60 Memorable Losses*?

I hope so. ■

James Altucher has written 25 books. About 21 of them are bad but one or two are OK. He has started several companies and has a popular podcast called 'The James Altucher Show'. Among others, Garry Kasparov and Judit Polgar have been guests on his podcast, as well as Kareem Abdul-Jabbar, Richard Branson and 963 others. He has played chess since he was 16 but stopped when he hit 2204 USCF in 1997, and is now starting to play again.

Garry Kasparov: 'Whether you spell Garry with a G or an H in Russian, you still pronounce it with a strong G. I was named after President Truman – Harry – whom my father admired for taking a strong stand against communism. It was a rare name in Russia, until Harry Potter came along.' *(The former world champion, in The Guardian's weekend lifestyle feature 'This much I know')*

Stevie Nicks: 'She taught me how to maneuver through life without people really knowing that I was so clever – so that I was just moving the chess pieces as I went. And nobody really knew that, but I was.' *(The Fleetwood Mac singer/songwriter and solo artist on her mother, interviewed in the February issue of The New Yorker)*

Ding Liren: 'A chess player, no matter if he is introverted or extroverted, has a very calm and steady side. When he is playing, he is able to concentrate on the board and think about the game and the possible changes.' *(Interviewed in February for China Global Television Network, the English-language arm of Chinese state media and television)*

Alfred Kreymborg: 'To the ignorant outside world, two men over a chessboard look like a pair of dummies. And yet, inside the pale automata, dynamos pound incessantly. Here is nothing less than a silent duel between two human engines using and abusing the faculties of the mind.' *(The early 20th-century avant-garde American poet, novelist and playwright was also a dedicated chess player)*

Veselin Topalov: 'Magnus should give his brain to science.' *(The Bulgarian's verdict on the Carlsen-Nepomniachtchi World Championship Match)*

Jon Ludvig Hammer: 'Wijk aan Zee is a windswept outpost in No Man's Land. It is a miracle that Magnus loves it. Probably has a lot to do with him winning pretty much every time he plays there.' *(On Norway's live TV coverage of the Tata Steel Masters on TV2 Sports)*

Lubosh Kavalek: 'Misha Tal was to chess what the saxophonist Charlie Parker was to jazz. Both flying high with no barriers, no limits to their intuition, imagination and improvisation.' *(The late chess columnist writing in his Huffington Post column on 6 October 2016)*

Gabriel Gatehouse: 'The Ukraine is a pawn in a game of chess where only one side is playing.' *(The BBC International Editor, speaking on the Ukraine crisis on Newsnight)*

Mats Wilander: 'He's [Medvedev] a chess player. He hits the shot that he thinks is right for the moment, not because of where the score is. He's just a really good tactician on the court as on the board.' *(The former Grand Slam champion-turned-analyst, previewing what turned out to be a truly epic Australian Open final between the Russian chess-mad Daniil Medvedev and Rafael Nadal, which the Spaniard won)*

Stefanos Tsitsipas: 'I'm trying to dictate play, see into the future if I do certain things, what's the next move? When I play chess I also get lost into the game and it's a beautiful thing to be able to zone in so much and be in the present moment.' *(The deep-thinking Greek tennis star, describing his five-set victory over Taylor Fritz in the fourth round of the Australian Open)*

Magnus Carlsen: 'I've enjoyed reading the books about old Soviet chess championships lately. Remarkably, a key part of that history is still alive and thriving. Happy 100th birthday!' *(A congratulatory tweet from the World Champion on Yuri Averbakh's 100th birthday)*

Albert Einstein: 'How can such a talented man devote his life to something like chess?' *(Speaking on his multi-talented friend, Emanuel Lasker)*

Arthur Koestler: '[Chess] is the perfect paradigm for both the glory and the bloodiness of the human mind.' *(Writing for the Sunday Times on the 1972 Fischer-Spassky match)*

The mysterious little yellow book

(And how to trick your opponent)

Mostly when we ask chess players to name a book that had a profound influence on them, they go for generally accepted classics. Not so **GREGORY SERPER**. Once a prominent Soviet grandmaster and nowadays a successful coach in Seattle, Serper tells the story of a most remarkable book that very few will know. It looks like a children's chess book, but what is it really?

The second part of September 1988 was quite memorable for me. I spent two weeks at a training camp near Moscow where, together with future super stars Ivanchuk, Gelfand and Dreev, I prepared for the coming World Junior Championship under 20 in Adelaide, Australia. It was not an easy task, since somehow my service in the Soviet Army hadn't really improved my chess abilities. I will never forget Alexey Dreev's eyes when we played a blitz game upon my arrival at the camp. He just said: 'What happened to you, Grisha?' Since it was a rhetorical question, he didn't wait for my response.

The first couple of days, my coach, Sergey Timofeevich Pinchuk, was giving me all kinds of tests trying to jump-start my chess abilities, but I failed most of them. It was very depressing, since the start of the World Championship was getting closer. Still, I didn't lose hope, because master Pinchuk was an excellent coach, who had made me a chess player, and I trusted his magic.

One day he took a small yellow book from his suitcase and put it on our desk. 'Chess Self-Tutor', I saw the title was. I took the book and opened the first chapter. I couldn't believe what I saw there. 'The evaluation of the initial position', 'A shelter for the king' and, as the cherry on top, 'The openings for beginners'. I couldn't hide my amazement. You see, at that point I wasn't a grandmaster and not even an International Master, but just a year before I had won the bronze medal in the World Junior Championship behind Anand and Ivanchuk, drawing both of them in the process... so I was not a beginner!

'Yes, I am in very bad form right now,' was all I could say at that moment, 'but a book for beginners, Sergey Timofeevich? Really??' My coach was a very wise person, so he didn't argue. Instead, he offered me a look at one of the positions from the book. It was not a tactical or positional exercise, just a position from a game that didn't look all that remarkable, at least to me. Then my coach read the text and I suddenly saw many hidden layers that had been invisible before and required some serious creativity to find. I instantly liked it and asked for more, so we started working with this book. Suddenly I could see some progress!

White to move

The author asks the reader to assess the position, think about White's and Black's threats. Who should defend against what? Or is it just a dead draw maybe?

we only have the primitive hope that Black will take the rook 1...fxe6? 2.fxe6+.

8. Therefore Black's queen leaves its ideal defensive post, but nevertheless Black is happy because he has the illusion that he has started a decisive attack!

In the game Stoltz-Tartakower, Bled 1931, after **1.♖e6 ♛d4 2.♚c6** Black played **2...♗b6** without much hesitation.

Indeed, since White has moved his major pieces away from the back rank, Black gets an opportunity to execute the attack he had been dreaming about for so long.

'Ivanchuk is a genius! He wasn't turned off by a book for beginners. He could see beyond the first chapter!'

At first, it was very little, but I could clearly feel that I was getting back into form. It was like acupuncture, when they stick a needle somewhere into your pinky and suddenly you feel a relief in your upper body. So we kept doing this 'chess acupuncture' till one day Vasily Ivanchuk was sitting in our room and noticed the book. He opened it, took a quick look and asked to borrow it for a couple of hours. After he left I couldn't contain my admiration. 'Ivanchuk is a genius!' I stated an obvious fact. 'He is in the top 20 in the world already, and yet he wasn't turned off by a book for beginners. He could see beyond the first chapter!'

My coach and I worked on other chess stuff, but three days later we decided to ask Ivanchuk to return the book, since we needed it for our own training.

You, my dear readers, are probably wondering what kind of positions were so fascinating that one of the best players in the world couldn't part with the book for three days. Well, here is a good example.

Then, in the solutions the author provides a long essay with elements of psychology, philosophy and basic common sense.

A very short summary of this essay would look like this:
1. Black would love to attack the f2-pawn by playing ...♖d2, followed by ...♛d4 and ...♗b6 (provided that the white queen or rook leave the back rank).
2. If both opponents are going to pay attention, then your evaluation of the position as drawish would be correct.
3. A true chess player will never accept that it is impossible to find something unusual in a position!
4. Experience teaches us that if you see no clear way to make progress by regular means, you need to use human factors.
5. Don't expect that if you set a primitive trap, your opponent will take the bait. Instead, you need to create an illusion that in the coming fight of ideas he will be smarter. Then there's a chance he will fall for it.
6. If the black queen leaves its post, we have the idea of a ♛a8-c6-g6+! And checkmate.
7. So, we play 1.♖e6!, pretending that

Now White suddenly returns to the back rank: **3.♖e8!!,** threatening ♛g6!, and checkmate follows.
Of course, Black saw it coming and he had a major card up his sleeve. He played:
3...♛xf2+ 4.♚h3 ♛f1+ 5.♚h4 ♗d8+ 6.f6+

6...g6 Now if White takes the rook, then after 7.♛xd7 ♗xf6+ 8.♚g4 h5 it's checkmate!
Black had even seen that if White plays

Two weeks later, Bronstein brought the same manuscript but with a different title

the desperate sacrifice 7.♗xg6+ ♔xg6 8.♕e4+ ♔xf6 9.♕e5+ he answers with a counter-check 9...♔g6+ and wins. Ironically, this is exactly what White was hoping for. Black had the illusion that he had outsmarted and out-calculated his opponent.

It is show-time now! White indeed sacrificed his bishop with **7.♗xg6+,** but after **7...♔xg6** he continued **8.♖g8+! ♔h7 9.♕e4+!!** and Black resigned, since after 9...♔xg8 10.♕g4+ ♔f8 he gets checkmated: 11.♕g7+ ♔e8 12.♕g8 mate.

I bet you would like to know who the author of this unusual book for beginners was. Haven't you guessed it yet? Of course it was one of the most imaginative and creative players in the history of our game, GM David Bronstein. Many years later, when we both played in a tournament in Oslo, I told him this story and thanked him for the excellent book, which had really helped me to prepare for the under-20 World Champion-ship. In the end Ivanchuk finished second there, and I got another bronze medal. In reality, Ivanchuk was supposed to be first and I should have taken second place right behind him. Unfortunately, a chain of weird events prevented the ultimate success of the players who had prepared with Bronstein's weird little yellow book for beginners.

Beginners?

During our conversation I couldn't resist a natural question: how is it a

book for beginners? Bronstein smiled and shared another amazing story of this little yellow book. When he brought his manuscript to the major Soviet publishing house Fizkultura i sport, he was told that the plan for books intended for advanced players was already complete.

I feel I need to elaborate for those of you who were not blessed enough to live in a socialist country. You see, our beloved Communist Party created five-year plans (known as *pyatiletka*) that decided how much meat, bread or pretty much anything under the sun we, the citizens of our great country, would need. And yes, each establishment had their own plans, which had to go along with the big pyatiletka plans. Failing or changing a plan would lead to severe consequences.

NEW IN CHESS

David Bronstein (1924-2006), one of the most brilliant players and thinkers the chess world has ever seen.

That's why the editor of the publishing house couldn't accept the brilliant manuscript of the legendary chess player and advised him to come back in a couple of years. 'But', the editor continued, 'if you wrote a book for beginners, we could publish it right away, since our plan for begin-ners' books has not been met yet.' 'Say no more!' Bronstein smiled. The editor smiled back. Yes, Soviet citizens knew the rules of the game. Two weeks later, Bronstein brought the same manuscript but with a different title. Also, at the very begin-ning of the book, a chapter for begin-ners was added.

Now, when you know the story of the book, you can really appre-ciate Bronstein's introduction. There he says that, while preparing this second edition, he had origi-nally intended to just add some new material to the first edition of his *Chess Self-Tutor*, which had been published seven years earlier. Unfor-tunately, while adding new material he got carried away, with the result that this second edition is completely different from the first one and can be regarded as the second part of his original book. If you can read between the lines of Bronstein's introduction, you'll see why the second edition of his *Chess Self-Tutor* is not a book for beginners!

Sheer stupidity

There is much wisdom in Bronstein's book, but the gem I like best is that 'experience teaches us that if you see no clear way to make progress by regular means, you need to use human factors.' It is so different from modern, heavily computerized chess. The thinking process of the majority of today's players can be summarized as 'I go here, he goes there'. But isn't the original goal of chess supposed to be an intellectual contest between two personalities? Where can you find the human factor Bronstein was talking about today? Call me old-fashioned, but trolling your opponent

Gregory Serper was born in the Soviet Union, in Tashkent (now Uzbekistan). In 1996 he moved with his family to the United States, a move he has never regretted.

Did you notice that? Black just played ...♖a7-a3-a7, then ...♖b7-b3-b7, then ...♖c7-c3-c7. So when Nimzowitsch tried ...♖d7-d3-d7, White prevented it by playing 49.♔e3!. This has nothing to do with real chess. Black is just goofing around, and White starts playing along. I am sure both opponents were smiling all along. In White's mind, the competitive part of the game was already over. Black is not even trying to make any progress, so why not have some fun? In the following part, Black just shuffles his rook around trying to find the most ridiculous place for it.

50.♖a5 ♔g6 51.♖g5+ ♔h6 52.♖a5 ♖b1 53.♖c5 ♖a1 54.♖b5 ♖a4 55.♖c5 ♖a8 56.♖b5 ♖h8!

Finally he finds it – the h8-square!
57.♖g5 Remember, psychologically White is playing along with Black's silly games, so he also finds a ridiculous square for his rook.

57...f5!! Oops, White's rook is trapped! **58.♔f4 ♖a8 59.♔e5 ♖a6 60.♔f4 ♖a4+ 61.♔e5 ♖e4+ 62.♔d6 g6 63.f3 ♖e3 64.g4 fxg4 65.fxg4 ♖g3 66.gxh5 ♖xg5 67.hxg5+ ♔xh5** 0-1.

by playing 1.f3 followed by 2.♔f2, or 1.e4 followed by 2.♔e2 is not a 'human factor'. It is sheer stupidity!

To find a real 'human element', let's look at another game played in a bygone era.

Oldrich Duras
Aron Nimzowitsch
San Sebastian 1912

position after 30.h4

The position is a relatively simple theoretical draw. Let's see how Aron Nimzowitsch uses the 'human element'.
30...♔h7 31.♖c7 ♔g6 32.♖a7 ♔f6 33.♖b7 ♖a5 34.♔g2 ♖a8 35.♔f3 ♖e8 36.♖b5 ♔g6 37.♖g5+ ♔h6 38.♖a5 ♖e7

So far, Oldrich Duras genuinely thought that his opponent was trying to improve his position to play for a win, but here something fishy is happening.
39.♖b5 ♖a7 40.♖c5 ♖a3+ 41.♔e2 ♖a7 42.♔f3 ♖b7 43.♖a5 ♖b3+ 44.♔e2 ♖b7 45.♔f3 ♖c7 46.♖b5 ♖c3+ 47.♔e2 ♖c7 48.♔f3 ♖d7 49.♔e3 ♖d1

Creating my own illusion

I feel this article would be incomplete if I didn't share my own game that demonstrates the wisdom that I learned from the small yellow book.

Andrei Shuraev
Grigory Serper
Kemerovo 1995

position after 47.♔g2

Here I spent about 20 minutes thinking about the position. In about two minutes it became clear to me that if my opponent completed his obvious set-up: ♔g3 and pawns f3, g4, h4, it would be a dead draw. The rest of the time I was looking for practical chances. The only idea I found consisted of two parts.

1. White pushes his pawn to h5 and allows me to play ...♔g5.

2. I bring my rook to f4, play ...f6-f5 and simplify into a winning king and pawn ending.

Unfortunately, both goals are unreachable. Indeed, how can I force him to play h4-h5? And even if I achieved the first goal, he would put his bishop on e4 and keep my rook from f4.

Fortunately, I remembered what Bronstein wrote in his book. You need to create the illusion that in the fight of ideas your opponent is smarter; then you will have a chance. Just like Gösta Stoltz gave Savielly Tartakower the illusion that Black could win. I thought that a similar strategy was my only chance.

So, what if I move my king far away? Then my opponent might think that by moving his passed h-pawn

he might get some winning chances. But where should I move my king? Moving it to a8 would be utterly stupid and therefore suspicious. So I decided to move it to e3. Yes, my king has no business there, but at least it creates the illusion that I am trying to attack his kingside pawns.

One more thing: if he pushes his pawn all the way to h7, he would indeed get winning chances by moving his king all the way to h6 and then g7. That's why, as soon as he moves h4-h5, I need to be able to play ...♖h8 to stop the dangerous pawn move to h6. And so, the first part of the 'mind games' has started:

47...♔e7 48.g4 ♔d6 49.h4 ♖b8!

Now I am ready to meet h4-h5 with ...♖h8!

50.♔g3 ♔d5 51.f3 ♔d4 52.h5? ♖h8!

I didn't even need to go all the way to e3, and he already played h4-h5. Should I move my king back to g5 now? No, that would be a huge mistake! My opponent would immediately smell a rat. Why would I change my plan and immediately move my king back home right after he played h5? So I decided to move the king all the way to e2 anyway. Clearly it has no other purpose than to create the impression that I was completing my original plan of moving my king towards White's pawns. Since this obviously doesn't yield any benefits, Black moves his king back out of desperation. Sounds quite believable!

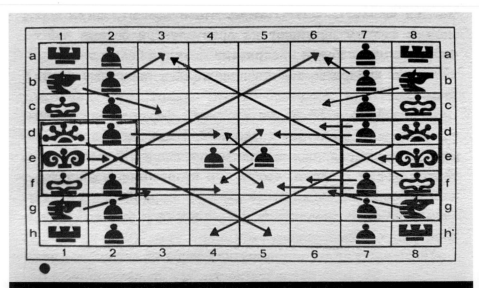

In the first edition of the little yellow booklet, Bronstein's originality also shone through in the diagrams (left to right!). In the second edition they were replaced by traditional diagrams.

**53.♗e4 ♚e3 54.♗f5 ♚e2!
55.♗e4 ♚e3**

Yes, it looks as if Black has realized the stupidity of his original plan and is moving his king all the way back.
56.♗f5 ♚d4 57.♗e4 ♚c5 58.♗f5 ♚d6 59.♚f2 ♚e7 60.♚g3 ♚f8 61.♗e4 ♚g7 62.♗f5 ♚h6 63.♗e4 ♚g5

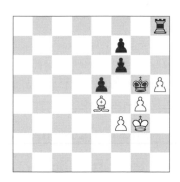

OK, the first step has been completed. Now we proceed to the second part.
64.♗d3 ♖a8 65.♗e4

What should Black play now? It is tempting to play 65...♖a4, hoping that White moves his bishop and then I play ...♖f4, winning on the spot. But this would be a huge mistake! My

opponent would think: 'Why, of all the squares on the a-file, would Black choose the a4-square? Then my plan would fail instantly. So, following in Nimzowitsch's footsteps, I started

No, let me ask it differently: what are the chances that your tired, annoyed opponent, who stopped paying attention a long time ago, notices the trap?

moving my rook anywhere except for the fourth rank!

At first, my opponent tried to find a hidden point behind my moves, but he obviously couldn't find one, because there wasn't any! After five or six completely pointless moves on my part he started paying less and less attention. After ten moves he was already sure that I was a loser who simply couldn't accept reality (i.e. a draw). So, when you play a dozen stupid moves and then suddenly play a move that contains a trap, what are the chances that your opponent notices the trap? No, let me ask it differently: what are the chances that your tired, annoyed opponent, who stopped paying attention a long time ago, notices the trap? Yes, that's the whole point!
65...♖a3 66.♗f5 ♖a5 67.♗e4 ♖b5 68.♗d3 ♖d5 69.♗f5 ♖d1 70.♗e4 ♖g1+

I think this stupid check is quite similar to Nimzowitsch's 56...♖h8!.
71.♚f2 ♖a1 72.♚g3 ♖a2 73.♗d5

♖a7 74.♗e4 ♖c7 75.♗d3 ♖c3 76.♗f5 ♖b3 77.♗c2
Now, when my rook is attacked, it must go somewhere. Why not the fourth rank then?

77...♖b4 78.♗e4!

Damn it, he stopped ...♖f4! Had he seen it, or was he just lucky?
78...♖d4 79.♗f5??
Yessss!
79...♖f4!

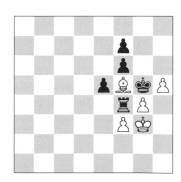

Now he realizes what has just happened, but it is too late!
80.♗e4 f5! 81.♗xf5 ♖xf5 82.gxf5 ♚xh5 83.f4 e4 0-1.

I think David Bronstein, who had the nickname 'Cunning Devik', would be proud to know how his little yellow book has helped me numerous times throughout my chess career! ■

MAGNUS CARLSEN TEACHES CHESS

Ruslan Ponomariov
Magnus Carlsen
Nice Amber Rapid 2010

position after 39.♖xa5

Winning the draw

He has a reputation of being a grinder, relentlessly pressing on in endings that others will only too readily agree to a draw. **MAGNUS CARLSEN** admits that he likes to fight by playing a game to its natural conclusion, as he takes us back to the 2010 Amber Rapid, where he reached a very equal ending against Ruslan Ponomariov...

There's no more equal position than this one: we have a symmetrical ♖+♙ ending with 4 v 4 on the kingside, and I think Ruslan offered a draw around this point. His only weakness I saw was the e5-pawn, as it's a little detached from his other pawns, so I thought I was a little better and decided to 'grind on'.

39...♖c4 Controlling the fourth rank and making it hard for my opponent to get f4 in.

40.♔g3 Perfectly fine, but he can go 40.g3 looking to support f4, and now if 40...g5 41.e6! f6 42.♖a8+ ♔g7 it's a draw by force, with a repetition after 43.♖a7 ♔f8 44.♖a8+ etc. The thing here is that even without the e-pawn we know it's a draw, but, psychologically, who wants to give up the e-pawn and try to hold a draw from a position of weakness?

40...e6 41.f4 h6

42.♔f3 Here he has his first little decision to make. If he tried 42.h4 I'm going to go 42...g5 and he'll probably have to take it twice with 43.hxg5 hxg5 44.fxg5 and I'm just going to play 44...♔g7. I can understand you are worried here as White that you are going to lose the g5- and e5-pawn, and then it is a different ball game.

42...♖c3+ 43.♔f2

He was faced with two options here, but I can't see what was wrong with 43.♔g4!. Now, it looks a little dumb, but if 43...h5+ he always has 44.♔h4, stopping ...♖g3, and there's nothing much I can do. But it probably just felt a little 'funny' to Ruslan, so he just retreated his king.

43...g5!

Nice, 2010, Ruslan Ponomariov vs. Magnus Carlsen. The opening was an Exchange Grünfeld that resulted in a dead equal position. But that was only the beginning…

Now I have something! He's either going to have to play g3 and I take on f4 and then capture on h3, or his e-pawn is going to be isolated. The game is still well within drawing range – but at least I have him thinking just a bit more.

44.fxg5 hxg5 45.♖a4

Once you get to this position with the e-pawn weak and a potential target, 9 times out of 10 you should still be

After all, I'm sure you wouldn't find 4 v 4 on the kingside in endgame books(!), so this is all relatively new territory

able to draw this – but you have given yourself a real task to hold.

45...♔g7 46.♖g4 ♔h6 47.g3

47...♔h5 There's nothing much happening for now – but instead if 47...♖c5, 48.♖e4 is probably something I don't want to allow, as 48...♔g6 49.g4 and that looks very solid. Once I start walking the king over to the queen-side with ...♔g6-g7-f8-e7-d7-c6, he's just going to play ♖e4-e3-f3, attacking the f7-pawn and that's going to be a big problem for me.

48.♖a4 ♔g6 49.♖a5 Now he doesn't want 49.♖g4, as I have 49...♔f5 followed by ...♖c5 and the e-pawn falls.

49...♖d3 If 49...♔f5 he has 50.♖a7. But objectively I have nothing, so I am just trying to confuse him, asking him the question with 49...♖d3. If he believes the threat is 50...♖d5 – of course it's nothing to worry about, because after 51.♖xd5 exd5 52.♔e3 ♔f5 53.♔d4

♔e6 54.g4! he has the better side of the draw. But I can understand the worry he might have had here, and it perhaps explains his next move.

50.h4?

It's all about pressurizing your opponent, have him make these little decisions/concessions by playing on when others would have agreed the draw – after all, I'm sure you wouldn't find 4 v 4 on the kingside in endgame books(!), so this is all relatively new territory, though it should be a very simple draw. And by continuing to play on, your opponent has to make moves, some decisions, which can be a bit difficult, as we'll see.

Instead, rather than the committal move 50.h4?, he should just have played the passing move 50.♖b5 to hold the draw.

50...gxh4 51.gxh4 The upshot of his committal move is that he was two weak isolated pawns and my pawns are still connected and strong.

51...♖d7

Nothing happens for the next dozen moves or so, we just manoeuvre around a bit... we're just waiting to see what happens.

52.♔e3 ♖b7 53.♔f4 ♖b4+ 54.♔g3 ♔f5 55.♖a7 ♖g4+ 56.♔f3 ♖g7 57.♖a5 ♖g1 58.♖b5 ♖a1 59.♖c5 ♖a3+ 60.♔f2 ♔e4

Once again I'm making some progress, because at some point he may run into little problems with ...♖f3+ and ...♖f5 hitting the vulnerable e5-pawn.

61.h5 ♖a8! Now it is all about that h-pawn being too far advanced, and my objective is to corral it.

62.♔g3 ♔f5 63.♔h4 ♖a4+ 64.♔g3 ♖g4+ 65.♔f3 ♖f4+ 66.♔g3 ♔g5 67.h6 ♖g4+ 68.♔f3 ♖h4

Finally I'm rewarded for my perseverance, as the h-pawn falls.

69.♖c7 ♔g6 70.♖c8 ♖xh6 I've won the h-pawn, though it is not yet a win – but now my opponent has to play very, very carefully.

71.♔g4?!

A step in the wrong direction, as we will soon see, as the king doesn't belong there. I guess the correct way to make the draw was 71.♖c7, let's say 71...♖h1 and just go 72.♔e4.

71...♖h1 72.♖g8+?

I guess this is the decisive mistake.

72...♔h7 73.♖a8 Originally he probably intended to play 73.♖g5 but that loses in a funny way to 73...♔h6! and the rook is lost to a ...♖g1, so he had to retreat with 73.♖a8.

73...♖f1!

Now my opponent is lost, as his king is cut-off. Luckily for me, a few years earlier I had a similar endgame win from a 4 v 3 pawns on the kingside, where I eventually cut off his king.

74.♖a2 ♔g6

75.♖g2 One possible line worth mentioning: if instead he defends the e5-pawn with 75.♖a5 then I have 75...♔f5 and ...f6! is winning.

75...♖f5 76.♖e2 ♔g7 As you can see, it takes a little time to convert, as I now have to march my king over to the queenside (ideally to d5) and then the e5-pawn falls.

77.♔g3 ♔f8 78.♖e4 ♔e7 79.♔g4 ♔d7 80.♖d4+ ♔c6 81.♖d6+ ♔c7 82.♖d1

He also had the trick move 82.♖d5, but once again winning was 82...f6!

82...♖xe5 Obviously, with two connected passers, the game now ends very quickly, though Ponomariov played on through inertia, finally resigning on move 100.

The lesson here in this example is that if you are the one with the weaker position, despite it looking a certain draw, you have to really concentrate on what you are doing. Once you have given your opponent real hope of making a win out of nothing, and you are in a position where you are not in a theoretical draw, the fact that you cannot force a draw is the real key. It means your opponent is going to be able to press for a long time – and those small concessions will build up and that only allows your opponent to play from a position of strength, pressing on and on. ∎

(This column is co-produced with Magnus Carlsen's 'Magnus Trainer' app. Download on Google Play, App Store, or visit playmagnus.com to read more lessons)

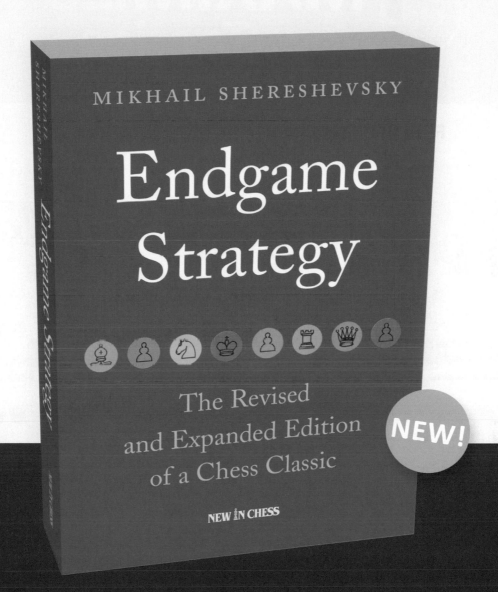

MAXIMize
your Tactics
with Maxim Notkin

Find the best move in the positions below

Solutions on page 86

1. Black to play

2. Black to play

3. Black to play

4. Black to play

5. White to play

6. Black to play

7. White to play

8. White to play

9. Black to play

GIBRALTAR
INTERNATIONAL CHESS FESTIVAL

#GibChess **Battle of the Sexes**: Men 53-47 Women

Congratulations to both teams on a magnificent performance!

sponsored by:

  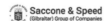  

Judit Polgar

Games and studies: a perfect match

It is no secret that **JUDIT POLGAR** is an ardent advocate of studies as a powerful tool to improve your game. Anyone eager to work on their endgame will benefit from endgame studies that seem to be 'cut from a real game'.

There are many good reasons why solving studies should be an important part of any player's training. While solving studies, you improve your calculating skills, your power of anticipating your opponent's defence moves, while also developing your imagination and fantasy.

Our reasoning becomes more concrete when we refer to the one-to-one connection between studies and practical endings. How many endings have been won or saved by using what commentators call 'study-like moves'? And how many studies feature such natural positions and play as if they were cut from a real game?

In practice, this means that solving studies on a regular basis also helps us to build a solid 'mental database' with miraculous ways of reaching the desired result. One never knows when such concrete knowledge will come in handy.

We will now examine a study-like endgame, in which Zsoka Gaal, the most promising young girl in Hungary

today, managed to save an apparently hopeless position.

Sheng-Gaal
Budapest 2021
position after 50.♖e1

Black's position looks joyless. She is two pawns down and her knight is dominated. With her next move, the 14-year-old Hungarian talent rightly considered that the pawn on a2 is edible.

50...♘xa2!
Passive defending will not save Black: 50...♖c3? 51.♖e4 ♖a3 52.♔f6 ♘xa2 53.♖d4, with a winning attack.
51.♖a1 ♖a4! 52.♗xa2

52.♗b3 ♖a3 does not change anything, while 52...♘c3 would free Black from the pin.

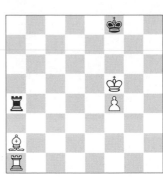

The game has entered a new phase. The pin along the a-file makes it difficult for White to make progress. There are two main winning ideas. The systematic way would be to find a safe square for the king, in order to advance the pawn all the way to f7. After that, the king would inevitably reach b2, removing the pin. During this process, Black could try to approach the pawn with her king. Since f7 is unavailable, this may offer White the second winning idea: if the king steps on e7 or g7, it could run into a freeing check from e1 or g1. The latter depends on the white king's position at that moment, of course.

52...♖a5+? Black's only mistake in this endgame, which remains more complicated than it may seem.

The correct defence was 52...♖a6!, putting White in zugzwang: 53.♔e5 (53.♔g5 ♔g7 is similar) 53...♔e7! (the point! White's king acts like a shield for its rival, since there is no check on e1) 54.f5 ♖a5+!. With a series of only moves, Black achieves a draw. Her king will now advance to f6, after which the f5-pawn will be lost.

It is worth mentioning that the zugzwang after 52...♖a6! is mutual. If it was Black to move, the king would have to stay on f8 and the rook would be forced to allow the white king's advance.

All smiles. Zsoka Gaal (14), the most promising girl in Hungarian chess, during a recent visit to Judit Polgar in her Budapest office.

53.♔g6? White chooses the wrong direction for his attack.

The young American GM should immediately have headed to the b-file with his king: 53.♔e6! ♖a6+ 54.♔d7 ♖a7+.

Accuracy is essential in the endgame. The king has to take the longest way to b2, since crossing the sixth rank too soon would allow Black to save the game with a nice trick: after

55.♔c6? ♖a4 56.f5 ♖a5 57.f6 ♖a6+ 58.♔d7 ♖xf6 59.♗g1,

ANALYSIS DIAGRAM

apparently, White is one step away from victory, but Black can use an elegant study-like idea to save the game: 59...♖g6!. The endgame is drawn, since 60.♗xg6 is stalemate! But after 55.♔c8! ♖a4 (with the e- and g-files clear, Black's king cannot move for the above reasons. 55...♖a5

56.♔b7 does not change much) 56.f5 ♖a6 57.♔b7 ♖a3 58.f6 ♖a4 59.f7 ♖a3 60.♔b6 the king goes to b2 unhindered and White wins.

53...♖a6+! The only way to prevent the pawn's advance.

In the event of a neutral move like 53...♖a7, White wins with 54.f5 ♔g7+ 55.♔h6 (55.♔f6 ♖f7+!? unnecessarily prolongs the variation) 55...♖a7 56.f6. After the pawn has reached f7, the king can navigate to b2 at its leisure.

54.♔h5 ♖a5+

The simplest way, but Black had an alternative in 54...♖a7 55.f5, the point being that after 55...♔g7 56.♖g1+ ♔f6 57.♗e6 Black wins the

How many endings have been won or saved by using what commentators call 'study-like moves'?

rook with 57...♖h7+ 58.♔g4 ♖g7+.
55.♔h4

55...♖a4!
Again the only move. Otherwise, White would play f4-f5.
56.♔g5 ♖a5+ 56...♔g7 was also possible, since the white king is shadowing the black one, preventing White from checking on g1.
57.f5 ♔g7
Black has achieved a safe set-up.

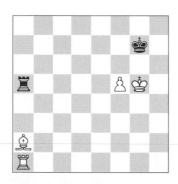

In chess studies, miracles come true...

58.♖b1 Alternatively, White could have gone for the rook and bishop versus rook ending with 58.♔f4.
58...♖xa2 59.♖b7+ ♔f8 60.♔g6 ♖g2+ 61.♔f6 ♔g8 62.♖b8+ ♔h7 63.♖e8 ♖f2 64.♔f8 ♖a2 65.♔f7+ ♔g8 66.♖e7 ♔f8 67.♖e6 ♖h2 68.♔g6

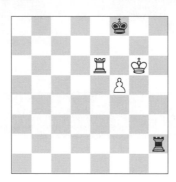

Draw.

There are a few elements that make this endgame similar to a study. The mutual zugzwang, the white king's optimal trajectory after Black's mistake, and the stalemate in the rook and bishop versus rook ending are a few of them.

We will now examine a study that features the same elements in slightly more refined forms. The study received the third commendation at the Chess Artistry Competition in Memory of Pal Benko during the Judit Polgar Global Chess Festival in Budapest last October.

Evgeny Egorov
3.c Chess Artistry Competition, 2021
White to move and draw

One can feel that in order to save the game, the white king needs to perform some miracles. In chess studies, miracles come true...
1.♔e2
1.♔f2? ♔d2, followed by ...♘e7, and the advance of the c-pawn wins easily. Now and later, White cannot allow the enemy king to step onto the d-file.
1...♔c2 2.♔e3 ♔c3

3.♔e4! Putting the knight under a partial domination.

The premature 3.g6? would lose to 3...♘e7 4.g7 ♘f5+ 5.♔e4 ♘xg7, and the knight will be in time to defend the pawn from e8.

3...♔c4 The kings advance shoulder to shoulder, maintaining the fighting dialogue across the d-file.

After 3...♘e7 4.♔e5 ♔c4 (preparing to sustain the knight on d5. In the event of 4...♘g6+ 5.♔d5, the c-pawn will be in danger) 5.♔f6 ♘d5+ 6.♔e5! ♔c5 7.g6 White draws with similar play as in the main line.

4.g6! Now that the king can no longer advance along the e-file, this is forced.

4...♔c5 5.g7 ♘e7 6.♔e5

The kings are continuing to shadow one another, but soon there will be some deviations.

6...♘g8 The most consistent try, aiming at restricting the white king's possibilities.

6...♔c6 would run into 7.♔e6! (the correct way to attack the knight, not allowing the decisive ...♔d7) 7...♘g8 8.♔f7 ♘h6+ 9.♔g6 ♘g8 10.♔f7, with an immediate draw.

7.♔e6 ♘h6!

Black is at a crossroads. A brief analysis shows that continuing his attack would give the black king time to reach a favourable position.

8.♔e5!!

For this reason, White does not need to continue his attack! Playing for zugzwang is the right approach.

8.♔f6? allows 8...♔d6, cementing the knight foothold on e7: 9.♔g6 ♘g8 10.♔f7 ♘e7, and Black wins.

A logical try (according to study terminology) is 8.♔d7? ♔b6! 9.♔e6 (9.♔c7 ♘f5+ wins) 9...♔c6! (this time it is White who finds himself in zugzwang) 10.♔f6 (10.♔e7 ♘f5+ and 10.♔e5 ♔d7 also win) 10...♔d7, with similar play as above.

Or if 8.♔e7, then 8...♔d5, with the same result.

8...♔c6 The best try. Moving the king away leads to an immediate draw: 8...♔b6 9.♔f6.

9.♔e6!

Renewing the zugzwang, which is in fact mutual, as is easy to establish.

9...♔c5 10.♔e5 c6

Black uses the reserve tempo to force the white king to abandon the opposition. Since this cuts off the black

king's retreat to c6, it does not yield the desired effect, though.

11.♔e6!

But not 11.♔f6, when 11...♔d6 wins.

11...♔d4 12.♔f6!

With the king far from d6, now is a good moment for this.

12...♔e4 13.♔g6 ♘f5!

The last try, since 13...♘g8 14.♔f7 leads to a repetition.

14.g8♘! In a good study, there is always a final touch!

14...c5 15.♘f6+

The newly born knight joins the battle just in time to ensure a draw.

Conclusions

■ When solving studies, it is a good idea to choose those with a natural starting position, as if taken from a game. Apart from developing general skills, this can provide valuable concrete endgame knowledge.

■ Whether solving or playing, finding the right idea does not mean having reached your final goal yet. One has to stay focused and alert to new critical moments, until the study has completely been solved or the game is over. ■

1. Arakhamia-Grant-Henriquez
Riga blitz 2021

With 25.♕c4? White pinned the black bishop, but it still controls square g1. **25...♖xh2+! 26.♔xh2 ♕h5+** White resigned in view of 27.♔g2 ♕h3 mate.

2. Nakamura-Svidler
chess.com speed 2021

With 28.♗c1? White hoped to win material, but... **28...♘2h3+! 29.♘xh3** If 29.gxh3 ♗d4+ and 30...♖d1+ mating. **29...♗d4+ 30.♔f2 ♖d1 31.♔f1 ♘e2+ 32.♔h1 ♖xf1** Mate.

3. Dubov-Aronian
chess.com speed 2021

24...♕h1+ 25.♔f2 g3+! (25...♕h4+ 26.g3+−) **26.♔e1** If 26.♔xg3 ♕h4 mate. **26...♕xf1+! 27.♔xf1 ♖h1** Mate.

4. Demchenko-Fedoseev
Riga FIDE Grand Swiss 2021

Black played 37...♘h5+ (and won), missing the gorgeous **37...♘e2+!** when 38.♕xe2 is met by 38...♕f4+ 39.♔h3 g4+ 40.♔h4 gxf3+ and 38.♔h2 ♕h7+! loses the knight.

5. Babazada-E.Mirzoev
Titled Tuesday 2021

31.♘e7+! ♗xe7 31...♖xe7 32.♕xh7+ ♔f7 33.♗g6 mate; 31...♔f7 32.♘xc6. **32.♕xh7+ ♔f8 33.♕h8+ ♔f7** Or 33...♗g8 34.♘h7 with a quick mate. **34.♗g6+! ♔xg6 35.♕h5** Mate.

6. Damljanovic-Ramoutar
Arandjelovac 2021

11...a4! 12.♕xb7 The only available square. **12...♗c5! 13.fxe5 ♘e7** Slowly but surely. **14.b3 ♖a7 15.♕xa7 ♗xa7** and Black was winning due to the imminent loss of the e5-pawn and the miserable positions of the white pieces.

7. A.Mastrovasilis-Trimitzios
Greece ch 2021

38.♘xf7+! ♖xf7 If 38...♔h7 39.hxg6+ ♕xg6 40.♕xe1 and Black is mated. **39.♕b8+ ♔h7 40.hxg6+ ♕xg6** 40...♔xg6 41.♕g8+ mating. **41.♖h3+ ♕h6 42.♖xh6+ ♔xh6 43.♕f4+! ♔h5 44.g4+** 1-0 (44...♔g6 45.♕f5+ ♔h6 46.♕h5 mate)

8. Janaszak-Jumabayev
Titled Tuesday 2021

19.♖xg7! ♕xf4+ The unprotected queen will be lost anyway: 19...♖xg7 20.♕g3+ ♔h8 21.♘g6+ or 20...♘g4 21.♘h5+. **20.♕xf4 ♔xg7 21.♕g3+ ♔h8 22.♕e5 ♔g7 23.♖e1** Black resigned.

9. Hong-Rahul
Charlotte 2021

25...♗xg2+! 26.♔xg2 On 26.♖xg2 ♕e3+ wins. **26...f3+! 27.♗xf3** After 27.♔xf3 ♕xg5 28.♕xc5 ♕xh5+ Black has a decisive attack. **27...♕xg5+ 28.♔h1 ♘xd6 29.exd6** and Black won easily.

Thomas Willemze

Club players, test your decision-making skills!

What would you play?

We all know the moments in a game when you don't know exactly what to do and how to proceed. Fortunately, there's something you can do almost always.

f you are in need for a plan during your game, focus on improving your worst-placed piece first. This is especially important when you have a cramped position and success depends on your ability to coordinate your army.

Exercises

The game between Andrzej Wasylk-iewicz (1811) and the young Bartlo-miej Niedbala (1546) – played in 2016 in the traditional Open in Polanica Zdroj, Poland – was a tough battle that started as a Caro-Kann but turned into a French structure in which Black had to find the right squares for his pieces. I created four exercises in which you can practise improving your worst-placed piece skills.

Exercise 1

position after 16.♘f3

Black has made a lot of progress on the queenside during the last couple of moves and is now ready to bring his knight into play. **What would you play?** Simply develop the knight with

16...♘e7, clear the f5-square first with 16...h5, or pressure White's centre with 16...f6, aiming for 17.exf6 ♘xf6 ?

Exercise 2

position after 28.♕e3

Which piece should Black improve? The knight, with 28...a4 and ...♘a5-c4, the light-squared bishop, with 28...b4 and ...♗b5, or the rook, with the elegant 28...♖c4 ?

Exercise 3

position after 29.♕f4

This position could have occurred in the game and again raises the ques-

tion of which piece needs improvement. **Would you play** 29...♘a5, 29...b4, or 29...♖c4 ?

Exercise 4

position after 47.♖c1

How should Black untangle his passive pieces? With 47...♔c8, 47...♔c6, or 47...♕a8 ?

I hope you enjoyed these exercises and were able to find the most effective improvement for your pieces. You can find the full analysis of this game below.

If you are in need for a plan during your game, focus on improving your worst placed piece first

Andrzej Wasylkiewicz (1811)
Bartłomiej Niedbala (1546)
Polanica Zdroj 2016
Caro-Kann Defence, Advance Variation

1.e4 c6 2.d4 d5 3.e5 ♗f5 4.g4 ♗d7

This is a very common manoeuvre in the Advance Variation of the Caro-Kann. Black pulls back the bishop within the pawn chain and opts for a French in which White already committed his g-pawn.

5.♗d3 e6 6.c3 c5

7.♕c2

White probably wanted to provoke a weakness on the kingside, but he should have focused on his development instead, with a move like 7.♘f3. In the game, he will soon end up in

White wanted to provoke a weakness on the kingside, but he should have focused on his development instead

trouble due to his lack of development and his vulnerable queen on the c-file.

7...♘c6!

Black simply ignores the attack on his h-pawn and increases the pressure on the white centre. This is a very typical response in these French positions.

8.♗e3 cxd4 9.♗xd4

9.cxd4 h5! followed by 10...♘b4 and ...♘xd3 would also have been very unpleasant for White.

9...♖c8!

10.♕e2 White loses another tempo with this move. 10.♕d1, to keep an eye on c1, would have been preferable.

10...♘xd4! 11.cxd4 ♖c1+ 12.♔d2 ♕c8 13.a3

13...a6

Black has played the opening very convincingly so far, but now hesitates for a moment. Both 13...♗a4, threatening ...♖d1+, and 13...♘e7 followed by ...h7-h5 and ...♘f5 would have been very pleasant for Black.

14.♖a2 g6 15.h4 ♖c7 16.♘f3

16...♘e7

Developing this knight is indeed a top priority, but Black should first address the upcoming h4-h5 push. The correct answer to **Exercise 1** was therefore 16...h5!, to simultaneously block the h-pawn and clear the f5-square for the knight.

16...f6 is another typical French move and would work out well after both 17.exf6 ♘xf6! and 17.h5 ♗h6+!, but White is not forced to act and will have a pleasant game if he maintains the tension with the simple 17.♘c3.

17.♘c3

17.h5! would have been more challenging for Black.

17...♘c6 18.♖aa1

Both players ignored a few opportunities to move their pawn to h5, and Black can be pleased that the fight is still taking place on 'his' queenside at the moment.

18...♘a5 19.♖ab1

This move loses a pawn, but 19.♔e3 ♘b3 20.♖a2 h5! wouldn't have been a picnic for White either.

19...♗xa3!

The b-pawn is responsible for protecting both a3 and c3 and is therefore overloaded.

20.♘a2 ♘b3+ 21.♔e3 ♗e7

22.g5! White is on his way to opening up the h-file with h4-h5xg6. **22...b5 23.h5 ♖f8 24.♔f4! ♕b7 25.♔g4**

After a long walk, the king has finally reached a safe square. It is now up to Black to create a breakthrough on the queenside, before White finds a way in at the other side of the board. **25...a5 26.hxg6 hxg6 27.♖h7 ♕b6 28.♕e3**

28...a4 This move facilitates the ...♘b3-a5-c4 manoeuvre and prevents the 29.♗xg6 tactic, but fails to solve Black's most urgent problem: his passive light-squared bishop. The correct answer to **Exercise 2** was to improve this worst-placed piece with 28...b4! and 29...♗b5. Now there is no need to fear 29.♗xg6, because Black will get a dream position after 29...fxg6 30.♕xb3 ♗b5. The third option, 28...♖c4, gives Black just enough compensation for the exchange, after 29.♗xc4 dxc4 30.♘c1!.

29.♖bh1 This move gives Black a second chance. 29.♕f4! was much stronger and would have brought us to **Exercise 3**.

ANALYSIS DIAGRAM

Black has to be very precise to stay out of trouble in this position. The point is that both 29...b4 and 29...♘a5 run into 30.♖xf7! ♖xf7 31.♗xg6, followed by 32.♗xf7 and a quick g5-g6-g7, with a winning advantage for White.
The remedy to this combination would be 29...♖c4!.

ANALYSIS DIAGRAM

Black can now meet 30.♖xf7 ♖xf7 31.♗xg6 with 31...♘xd4!. The game would probably have continued 30.♗xc4 dxc4 31.♖bh1 ♗c6, followed by ...♕b7, ♗e4 and ...♗f5, with excellent compensation for the exchange. **29...♔d8**

30.♕f4 This move has lost its effectiveness, because Black will be in time to protect f7.

30.♖h8! would have kept the game level.
30...♗e8 31.♖h8 ♖xh8 32.♖xh8 ♔d7! 33.♘c3

33...♖c4
Black has successfully neutralized the dangers on the kingside during the last couple of moves but now allows his opponent back into the driver's seat.
33...♖xc3! would have been a much stronger exchange sacrifice, turning his a-pawn into a deadly passer after 34.bxc3 a3 35.♘e1 a2 36.♘c2 b4!.
34.♗xc4 bxc4 35.♘xa4 ♛a5 36.♘c3 ♛b4

37.♛h2 White is in excellent shape after this move, but improving his worst-placed piece with 37.♘xd5! exd5 38.e6+! fxe6 39.♘e5+ would have been even more convincing.
37...♘c1 38.♛h7

Constantly improving your pieces is the key to sound positional play

38.♘xd5 exd5 39.e6+ was still very strong.
38...♛xb2 39.♛g8 ♛b8

40.♘b5
The most accurate move would be 40.♘a4!, after which Black cannot prevent ♘b6 because the queen is occupied defending the e8-bishop.
40...♗b4 41.♘d6 ♗xd6 42.exd6 ♘d3 43.♛f8 ♛d8 44.♘e5+ ♘xe5+ 45.dxe5 c3

46.♖h1!
I really like this switch. The rook is no longer needed on h8 and is on its way to stop the black pawns or attack the black king from the queenside.
46...d4

47.♖c1

This logical move spoils White's advantage. 47.♖a1! was required. Rooks are poor blockaders and should rather focus on attacking. White wins after 47...♔c6 48.♖a7!, followed by d6-d7.
47...♔c6!
Well played! Black solved **Exercise 4** and found the only move that keeps the game level. The king is heading for a safer location, from where it can support its passed pawns. Both 47...♔c8 48.♖a1! and 47...♖a8 48.♛e7+ ♔c6 49.d7! ♗xd7 50.♛d6+ are winning for White.
48.♔f3 This move could have got White into trouble. 48.♖a1 was still the way to go, leading to a perpetual after 48...c2 49.♔f4 d3 50.♔e3 ♛xg5+ 51.♔xd3 ♛f5+.
48...♔d5 49.♛h8

49...♛xg5
Black pulls the emergency brake and goes for perpetual check. A pity, because he could have crowned his king's march with 49...♔c4!. The king is completely safe at c4 and Black is winning after 50.♛h4 ♛b6 followed by ...♛b2 and ...c2.
50.♛xe8 ♛h5+ 51.♔g2 ♛g5+ 52.♔f3 ♛h5+ 53.♔g2 ♛g5+ 54.♔h2 ♛h5+ 55.♔g3 ♛g5+
Draw.

Conclusion
Constantly improving your pieces is the key to sound positional play. I hope this game enriched your arsenal of effective piece manoeuvres and reminded you that it's good to take your king for a walk every once in a while. ■

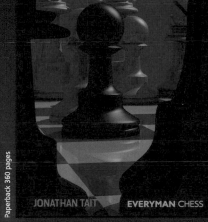
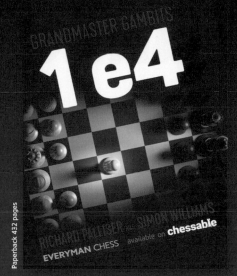
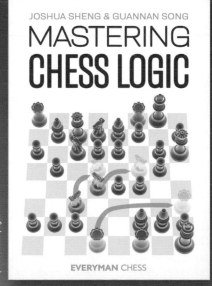
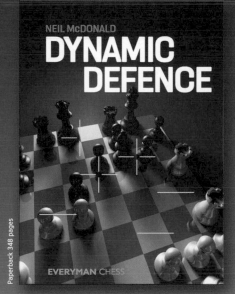

Working at your weaknesses

Are you an 'Activist', a 'Theorist', a 'Reflector' or a 'Pragmatist'? Probably, like most modern players, you are a blend of two or more of these categories. Nevertheless **MATTHEW SADLER** believes that if you are working at your shortcomings it makes sense to divide the great champions in such camps and view them as enlightening illustrations of the skills they are associated with.

The chess world never stops! It's only been a couple of months since Magnus Carlsen retained his World Championship title but it already feels like a distant memory after the drama of the World Blitz and Rapid championships in Warsaw and the Tata Steel Chess Tournament in Wijk aan Zee.

Perhaps the abiding impression of the Carlsen-Nepomniachtchi match is nothing to do with specific moves or preparation, but rather a psychological one: the difficulty in changing the type of player you are and the tendency of your weaknesses to rear their head under stressful situations. Nepomniachtchi did a super job in many respects, but the big worry before the match – that Ian's resilience to setbacks was markedly inferior to Magnus's – proved to be the defining factor.

Working at your weaknesses is of course something that every (professional) chess player does, but embedding this corrective work into your practical play is akin to changing a wheel on a moving vehicle. Practical success is often the result of a personal (unique) blending of skills that opponents find difficult to deal with. Improving an area of your game can alter that delicate balance and even lead to a drop in strength. For example, working at your positional game increases your awareness of the long-term risks your natural aggressive game entails. This new awareness inhibits your subsequent risk-taking, which means you put your opponent under less pressure... and the flow of wins you took for granted starts to dry up.

Continually thinking about your weaknesses is also a dangerous approach for practical players. At some stage you have to believe in yourself and impose your strengths on your opponents. After all, the best way to hide your weaknesses is to guide your opponent towards fighting against your strengths.

So there are two possible pitfalls: you might affect the strength of your overall game by tinkering with improvements, and you might reduce your confidence during practical play by excessive focus on your weaknesses. It's often useful in such cases to shift the focus away from yourself and consider things more generally. For example, comparing yourself to other players with similar skillsets and understanding their strengths and weaknesses is a less confrontational way of identifying useful areas of your game to work on, and avoids blaming yourself unnecessarily for chess failings (because other people have them too!).

This last observation made me extremely interested in *The 4 Player Types standard model* by Karsten Müller and Luis Engel (ChessBase DVD). This DVD builds on a 2005 work by Lars Bo

The best way to hide your weaknesses is to guide your opponent towards fighting against your strengths

Hansen called *Foundations of Chess Strategy* (Gambit), which categorised players into 'Activists', 'Reflectors', 'Pragmatists' and 'Theoreticians' (I tried to get hold of this now out-of-print book but quoted prices of $80-$200 sort of put me off!).

A couple of these titles are intuitive, a couple need some explanation to make sense of them. The DVD takes them one by one, Karsten Müller examining the 'Activists' (Alekhine, Kasparov) and the 'Theorists' (Steinitz, Botvinnik, Kramnik), and Luis Engel braving the 'Reflectors' (Petrosian, Karpov, Carlsen) and 'Pragmatists' (Euwe, Lasker, Fischer). In each category, the authors draw general conclusions about the tendencies, strengths and weaknesses of the associated players. It's the beautiful thing about chess and the strong characters of our World Champions that I'm sure you already have some feeling for the categories just by seeing the names attached to them! For example, you see Karpov in the 'Reflectors' category and you know that deep strategic understanding of the game and intuition is a part of that skillset.

A quick example (one of my all-time favourites!)

Slim Bouaziz
Anatoly Karpov
Hamburg 1982

position after 25.♔f2

25...♘b8
'A little early to start setting up the pieces again!' was the comment on Twitter after I shared this example!

The 4 Player Types standard model
Karsten Müller & Luis Engel
ChessBase DVD, 2021
★★★★☆

It's a beautiful move, regrouping the knight from c6 to c5. Why not activate the rook on a8 before doing so? Karpov has a plan!
26.♘f3 ♘d7 27.♔g3 ♘c5 28.♖d1 a5 29.♔f2 ♖a6

That's it! Karpov had envisaged activating the rook on the 6th rank!
30.♔e2 ♘a4 31.d4 ♖b6 32.dxe5 ♖xb2+ 33.♔f1 ♘xc3 34.exd6 cxd6 35.♖xd6 ♖b1+ 36.♘e1 ♔f6 37.♖d2 b5 38.♘c2 b4 39.♔f2 ♖a1 40.e5+ ♔xe5 41.♘f3+ ♔e4 42.♘d4 ♔d3 0-1.

My feelings about the value and accuracy of these models varied significantly while watching the videos, but I eventually settled into an appreciative mood! Perhaps that's an indication that you have to get clear in your own head what you can get out of these models and what their strengths and limitations are. Once you do that, however, I think that they can be of significant practical value.

To start with, you mustn't take them too literally. In the modern era where elite players are significantly more universal than 'classical' players (that tag unfortunately includes

players of my era!), assigning them to one category can feel like hammering a square peg into a round hole, and makes you want to take issue with the authors' choices! However, it's more useful to view these players as illustrations of skills in this category (for example, no one would question that Magnus is a great exponent of the 'Reflector' qualities) rather than bounded by the category.

A related point is that you can intuitively (wrongly) assume that categories are exclusive, which can be confusing when the category role models are so strong. I guess I was a 'Theorist' as a professional player (someone who knew his systems and the associated middlegame schemes intimately and who liked clean games with a single dominating theme), but it's pretty clear that Magnus would be much stronger than me in this category too!

A quick example of typical 'Theorist' play would be Botvinnik's famous victory against Alekhine at the 1938 AVRO tournament.

Mikhail Botvinnik
Alexander Alekhine
Amsterdam 1938
1.♘f3 d5 2.d4 ♘f6 3.c4 e6 4.♘c3 c5 5.cxd5 ♘xd5 6.e3 ♘c6 7.♗c4 cxd4 8.exd4 ♗e7 9.0-0 0-0 10.♖e1 b6?

A bad opening mistake from Alekhine, that allows Botvinnik to switch the battle from a fight around White's isolated queen's pawn to a fight along the open files adjacent to the isolated queen's pawns. This new

fight is clearly to White's advantage: White already has a rook on the e-file while 10...b6 has weakened Black's control of c6 making it impossible to maintain a piece barrier on the c-file. **11.♘xd5 exd5 12.♗b5 ♗d7 13.♕a4 ♘b8 14.♗f4 ♗xb5 15.♕xb5 a6 16.♕a4 ♗d6 17.♗xd6 ♕xd6 18.♖ac1**

It couldn't be clearer that White is better equipped for the fight ahead. In particular, the c-file is a fruitful invasion channel for White's rook right to the end of the game.
18...♖a7 19.♕c2 ♖e7 20.♖xe7 ♕xe7 21.♕c7 ♕xc7 22.♖xc7 f6 23.♔f1 ♖f7 24.♖c8+ ♔f8 25.♖c3 g5 26.♘e1 h5 27.h4 ♘d7 28.♖c7 ♖f7 29.♘f3 g4 30.♘e1 f5 31.♘d3 f4 32.f3 gxf3 33.gxf3 a5 34.a4 ♔f8 35.♖c6

It's a nice touch that the c6-square weakened on move 10 is still being exploited 25 moves later!
35...♔e7 36.♔f2 ♖f5 37.b3 ♔d8 38.♔e2 ♘b8 39.♖g6 ♔c7 40.♘e5 ♘a6 41.♖g7+ ♔c8 42.♘c6 Even 32 moves later!
42...♖f6 43.♘e7+ ♔b8 44.♘xd5 ♖d6 45.♖g5 ♘b4 46.♘xb4

axb4 47.♖xh5 ♖c6 48.♖b5 ♔c7 49.♖xb4 ♖h6 50.♖b5 ♖xh4 51.♔d3 1-0.

Finally, some part of you always rebels at being categorised! A category doesn't take account of all your skills or of your development as a chess player. For example, in many positions I act more like an 'Activist' (someone who values the initiative and attacking chances above material – probably my first instinct before my brain kicks in to keep me sensible) or a 'Pragmatist' (which Engel defines as concrete players who like to calculate lines and base their actions not on intuition but on specific variations).

And yet for all that, it's a very interesting and worthwhile exercise to hold your play up to a set of chess and psychological characteristics gleaned from great players and see how it compares! For example, I was struck by Müller's insight that 'Activists' often make weakening pawn moves without taking proper account of the downsides and that they often defend poorly when passive defence is required. He illustrates this with a game of Kasparov's (the greatest 'Activist' of all time!) against Kramnik from their World Championship match in 2000.

Vladimir Kramnik
Garry Kasparov
London 2000 (2nd match game)

position after 34.♖b4

34...♖d7 34...♗d6 35.♖c4 ♖a5 was the best chance to defend this (unpleasant) endgame according to Müller. Kasparov manages to lose this endgame within six moves by what Müller calls 'pseudo-activity'.

35.♔g2 ♖d2+

These are active attacking moves, but there is no attack in the position!

36.♔h3 h5

Müller points to this too as typical of Activists – making aggressive pawn moves but not taking account of the downsides. This pawn move feels as if it might help Black with a counter-attack against White's king by taking away the g4-square, but this counter-attack is simply never going to materialise. Black therefore essentially brings one of his pawns closer to White's position, making it easier for White to attack it.

37.♖b5 ♔f6 38.a5 ♖a2 39.♖b6+ ♔e7 40.♗d5

And Kasparov resigned.

40...♖xa5 41.♖e6+ ♔d7 42.♖xe5 ♔d6 43.♖xh5 (picking up the h-pawn on the way now it has been pushed to h5) 43...♖xd5 44.♖xd5+ ♔xd5 45.♔g4 wins.

Obviously Kasparov was not

Understanding this from the mistakes of others is much less painful than staring at the ruins of your own handiwork!

in his best shape for this match (probably partially caused by Kramnik's stellar play and psychological insight) but I suddenly realized that I have defended positions in a similarly 'pseudo-active' manner on a number of occasions. Understanding this from the mistakes of others is much less painful than staring at the ruins of your own handiwork! The power of such models also lies in facilitating general reflections on how – for example – you as a 'Theorist' should approach a game against a 'Pragmatist'.

In summary, I think this DVD is worth a serious look and I think that some players might get a lot out of it! I suppose the one thing I was somewhat nonplussed about was that there didn't seem to be a common structure to the 4 categories: the 'Activist' section is huge and is divided up into an Introduction, Endgames, Strengths and Weaknesses, but the other chapters are not so well-structured. However, in general really interesting and got me thinking – 4 stars!

■ ■ ■

The Secret Ingredient to Winning at Chess by Jan Markos and David Navara (Quality Chess) is probably a book I would recommend as a companion to Müller and Engel's DVD! At least, I read them one after the other and it was lovely to see such contrasting approaches to thinking about chess. Whereas Müller and Engel are all about models and cate-

gories, Markos and Navara are all about personal, practical experiences and insights.

Markos – the main author – explains in his introduction how he lost a critical last-round game in a World Youth Championship. 'Looking back now, I'm not surprised that I lost. I might have been a gifted chess player back then, but I was not aware of the secret ingredient needed to succeed in chess: I knew almost nothing about practical aspects of a chess fight. I had no idea how to prepare for an opponent or how to control my emotions. And I knew absolutely nothing about how a crucial game should be played. This is above all a practical book. My goal is simple: I want to help you avoid as many disastrous defeats as possible... In short, this book wants to teach you how to win at chess.'

To this end, Markos takes us through chapters with names such as 'An Ordinary Day at Work' (what grandmasters think about at the board), 'Coming of Age' (the difficult and crucial skill of defence), 'I Feel, Therefore I am' (examining the crucial role that emotions play at the board) and 'A Treat for the Opponent' (how to serve your opponent the opening line that will not taste good to him at all). Markos is the main narrator, with Navara chipping in with remarks and comments from his experience.

I learnt – sometimes rediscovered – many great practical tips from this quirky and original book. One I really liked in particular was Navara's comment when asked to what extent it is possible to employ tailor-made preparation against a specific opponent. Navara replies that 'A player who is familiar with many openings and is comfortable in all kinds of positions will be able to apply targeted preparation for an opponent much more efficiently than someone with a narrower repertoire. **Versatility and psychology go hand**

The Secret Ingredient to Winning at Chess
Jan Markos &
David Navara
Quality Chess, 2021
★★★★☆

and hand in chess. If you want to use psychology, improve the versatility of your own style first'. For me that's the best thing that's ever been said about this subject!

Obviously, my attention was also drawn to the chapter on engines entitled 'One Number is Not Enough'. It's a bit churlish of me to complain about this, as there is nothing wrong with the main thrust of the chapter – that engine evaluations often do not reflect the human playability of a line and that you should use your judge-

I learnt – sometimes rediscovered – many great practical tips from this quirky and original book

ment when deciding to follow the engine or not.

However, a couple of details sprang out to me in the chapter. Firstly, Markos uses Stockfish 9 (on just 3 threads which is an extremely modest configuration) to generate examples of (bad/dubious) engine evaluations. We are now up to Stockfish 14.1 and a huge architectural change further (since Stockfish 12) so it seems really strange to use an engine released in February 2018 as the reference in 2021. I have noticed a tendency to view engines as a standard, fixed tool like a hammer or wrench, but this is far from the truth – they are continually evolving software, and professional chess players really need to keep pace with them.

A second point arises when Markos discusses the position that arose in the game Lupulescu-Navara, Antalya 2017.

Constantin Lupulescu
David Navara
Antalya 2017

position after 60.♔c4

Anyone who knows their fortress positions will recognize this one as a draw (I even drew this ending at the age of 12 against then IM Dave Norwood!) and Markos concludes by saying: 'My computer, by the way, evaluates the position as +6.72.' It's absolutely true that engines still struggle with some fortress positions, but it also depends a bit which engine you consult. Leela Zero for example says off the bat that the position is equal (an evaluation of +0.07). Even if you add two extra h-pawns on h3 and h4 (which confuses engines much more than us!) Leela's evaluation still suggests a draw.

The conclusion is that one part of the skill of using engines is to understand which type of engine to use for different types of positions. Stockfish is unparalleled at tactical endgames (I have analysed some brilliant examples on my YouTube Silicon Road site) but Leela Zero's larger neural network is pretty impressive at understanding fortresses.

That was my only gripe however! For the rest a really interesting and original work, just like Markos' previous book *Under the Surface*! 4 stars! ■

They are The Champions

The 2021 champion of Uruguay is IM Bernardo Roselli Mailhe. Roselli won his first National Championship at the age of 19 and now, 37 years later, he clinched a record-breaking 29th title. The championship was played from November 22 to December 2 in Montevideo, the capital of Uruguay. Bernardo finished clear first with 7½ out of 10, half a point ahead of CM Facundo Vázquez Furtado and IM Nahuel Diaz Hollemaert.

Bernardo has been rated between 2400 and 2450 for over 20 years, but is not concerned that age will impact his strength. He never pursued the GM title, as his focus has been on building the chess community in Uruguay and South America. Bernardo lives by two mottos: 'Try every day to be better than yesterday' and 'You are your own worst enemy'. These values, taking responsibility for your continuous improvement, have been essential ingredients for his long-term success.

Roselli was born in the city of Carmelo in 1965. He was part of a large family, with five brothers and three sisters. His passion for chess came from his father, Diego Roselli Barilari, who was chess champion of Carmelo from 1964 to 1978.

Between 1986 and 2018, Bernardo participated in thirteen Chess Olympiads. At the 2018 Chess Olympiad in Batumi, Georgia, he was surprised when Susan Polgar contacted him after Round 9 on account of him winning the 'Game of the Day' award for his winning combination against Nenad Sulava.

In **They are The Champions** we pay tribute to national champions across the globe. For suggestions please write to editors@newinchess.com.

BERNARDO ROSELLI

Uruguay

But nothing will top the experience of playing Viktor Kortchnoi at the 2008 Dresden Olympiad in the match between Switzerland and Uruguay. Kortchnoi was 77 at the time and had the white pieces. A big crowd surrounded the board to watch the legend play. Petra Leeuwerik took good care of Viktor and supplied him with food and drinks. The Swiss coach, Artur Jussupow, watched the game intensely from the side. After 5.5 hours of play and 79 moves, the game ended in a draw. Roselli had been defending most of the game, but Kortchnoi could not break through his stubborn defence. Viktor Kortchnoi's energy and passion for chess ('Chess is My Life') have been an inspiration for Bernardo ever since.

Bernardo Roselli is the patriarch of Uruguayan chess. He was President of the Uruguayan chess federation for 12 years, organized many tournaments – including the World Junior in 2017 – and

has been a representative for FIDE and the Ibero-American Chess Federation. Bernardo also wrote a book about his country's chess history, *Traveling through Uruguayan chess 1980-1989*.

Roselli played one of his best games in 2001 in Montevideo, in the Uruguayan Championship, winning the game with a beautiful queen sacrifice.

Roselli-Crosa
Uruguayan Championship 2001
position after 20...♖a3

21.♗xf6 ♗xf6 22.♘xd5 ♖xd3 23.♘xf6+ ♔f8 24.♘xe8 ♖d2 25.♖b8 ♕xb8 26.♘d7+ ♔xe8 27.♘xb8 c5 28.dxc5 ♘e6 29.c6 ♔d8 30.♘d7 ♔c7 31.♘f6 ♘c5 32.g3 ♘d3 33.♘d5+ ♔c8 34.♖a1 1-0.

Bernardo currently works as a chess teacher at schools, and coaches talented youth. His focus continues to be the growth of chess in Uruguay and throughout the South-American continent. He believes it is crucial to convince more people outside the chess world of the educational value of chess.

Furthermore, it is his dream to have Uruguay organize the Chess Olympiad in 2028, within the framework of the FIFA World Soccer Championship held in Uruguay, Argentina, Chile, and Paraguay in 2030. ∎

Jan Timman

Yuri Averbakh celebrates 100th birthday

Yuri Averbakh became the first grandmaster ever to reach the venerable age of 100. In his rich life, Averbakh had a wide variety of roles in the Russian and international chess community. In his tribute **JAN TIMMAN** looks at the world-class player and endgame specialist.

The indestructible Yuri Averbakh turned 100 years old on February 8th, a milestone that no grandmaster before him has ever reached. Last summer Averbakh was hospitalized with corona, but he survived and following a one-month stay in a recovery centre (courtesy of the Russian Chess Federation), he returned home again. In his apartment in Moscow, he still enjoys working on chess, but is restricted by poor eyesight and loss of hearing.

The chess world knows Averbakh as a man with many faces. In random order: arbiter, second, historian, author, official, endgame theoretician, and above all: player. In 1954, he won the Soviet Championship with the amazing score of 14½ out of 19, proof that he was an absolute top player. When in an interview for Chess.com, Peter Doggers asked him what he regarded as his greatest achievement, Averbakh surprisingly enough mentioned his book *A History of Chess – from Chaturanga to the Present Day*, published by Russell Enterprises in 2012. You can understand why he preferred this book over his standard works on endgame theory, though. These days, endgame theory is determined by computers, which has made the standard works largely superfluous. Chess history, on the other hand, is still largely uncharted territory. On this occasion, however, I still want to highlight his achievements as an endgame theoretician and player.

Last summer he was hospitalized with corona, but Averbakh survived

Averbakh's tendency to liquidate to clear technical endgames already manifested itself in his early games. An example is his game against Andor Lilienthal, who was the oldest grandmaster alive for many years and died three days after his 99th birthday in 2010. Twice, Averbakh goes for simplifications to steer the game into endgame-theoretical waters. According to *Averbakh's Selected Games*, the game was played in 1948, but that is incorrect – there was no Moscow championship in that year.

Yuri Averbakh
Andor Lilienthal
Moscow 1949
King's Indian Defence

1.d4 This was just the second time in Averbakh's career that he opened with the queen's pawn. He was an inveterate 1.e4-player.
1...♘f6 2.c4 d6 3.♘f3 g6 4.♘c3 ♗g7 5.e4 0-0 6.h3

It was five years later that Averbakh would introduce his variation – with ♗e2 and ♗g5 – but what he plays here is also good, of course.
6...♘c6 Dubious. Black is wasting precious time.
7.d5 ♘b8 8.♗e2 e6 9.0-0 exd5 10.exd5 The alternative 10.cxd5 would also have yielded a plus. But Averbakh keeps the position as transparent as possible.
10...♖e8 11.♗e3 ♘bd7 12.♖c1 Inaccurate. With 12.♗d3 or 12.♖e1 White could have retained his plus.

12...♘c5

Ulf Andersson wouldn't have hesitated: 12...♖xe3! is an excellent exchange sacrifice. After 13.fxe3 ♕e7 White has a choice: giving up his e-pawn – and allowing Black excellent compensation – or settling for 14.♕d2 ♗h6 15.♘d1, followed by 15...♘c5, with strong pressure on White's position.

13.♘d4 ♘fe4 14.♘xe4 ♘xe4 15.b3 ♘g3 16.♖e1 ♘xe2+ 17.♖xe2 ♗d7 18.♕d2 a6 19.♖ce1 ♕h4 20.♘f3 ♕h5 21.♗d4 ♖xe2

22.♕xe2

Averbakh correctly indicates that 22.♖xe2 would have been stronger. It looks as if there's a problem, since Black can capture on h3, but this won't work in any variation. The main line continues as follows: 22...♗xd4 23.♕xd4 ♗xh3 24.♖e4 ♗d7 25.♖h4 ♕f5 26.♖f4 ♕b1+ 27.♔h2 h6 28.♕f6 ♖f8 29.♕e7 g5 30.♖f6! ♕b2 31.♖xh6 ♕g7 32.♕xg5, and White has a healthy extra pawn. This line is not very difficult, but Averbakh probably didn't go into it very deeply, since he wanted to play an endgame.

Yuri Averbakh loved to travel. This photo was taken in Australia in 1967.

22...♗xd4 23.♘xd4 ♕xe2 24.♖xe2 ♔f8 25.f3 c5

Averbakh is a bit unhappy with this move. He writes: 'Here the centralized knight is stronger than the bishop, the mobility of which is severely restricted. Therefore, Black tries to open lines, but in so doing he worsens his pawn structure.'

This comment shows how dogmatically Averbakh sometimes looked at positions. The text is the computer's first move – it's important to create more space, and a weak but easily defended pawn will not cause any problems.

26.dxc6 bxc6 27.♖d2 ♔e7 28.♘e2 ♗e6 29.♔f2

29...d5?

A strange strategic error for a player of Lilienthal's calibre. He appears to have been unfamiliar with the game Botvinnik-Konstantinopolsky, Sverdlovsk 1943.

30.c5

The same structure and material ratio as in Botvinnik's game. White is strategically winning.

30...♔d7 31.♘d4 f6 32.♖e2 ♗f7 33.f4 ♖g8 34.g3 h5 35.♖e3 ♖e8

Sergey Janovsky, the head coach of the Russian Chess Federation, visited Yuri Averbakh on his birthday. He brought gifts, congratulatory messages and honoured the centenarian with the Golden Badge of the RCF.

36.♖xe8!

This exchange is completely justified. The endgame of knight against bad bishop is winning.

36...♗xe8 37.g4 hxg4 38.hxg4

38...♔c7

Averbakh observes that 38...g5 would have been more tenacious. But White still wins easily with 39.f5. The plan is simple: White takes his king to a5, forcing the black king to protect the queenside. Then the knight penetrates to h7 via e6 and f8. If Black advances his d-pawn, the white king returns to stop it.

39.♔g3 ♗d7 40.g5 fxg5 41.fxg5 ♗c8

Here the game was adjourned, and later resigned by Lilienthal without resuming play. The white king will penetrate decisively.

Birth of a passion

Averbakh's interest in theoretical endgames had been aroused three years earlier. In the Preface to *Comprehensive Chess Endings*, Volume I, he writes: 'In 1946 I, together with David Bronstein, was playing in a USSR Championship semi-final in Leningrad. On one of the free evenings David called in to show me the position from his adjourned game with Mark Taimanov. Incidentally, in those distant times we were young masters, merely dreaming about the chess heights. The position proved to be extremely interesting, and I enthusiastically began to analyse it. We succeeded finding in it some exceptional, genuinely study-like possibilities.'

So this is how it started, five years before I was born. Later, Averbakh published his conclusions in *Shakhmaty v SSSR*. In Harold van der Heijden's database it looks like this:

Yuri Averbakh
Shakhmaty v SSSR 1948
White to play and win

This was the position in the adjourned game. Taimanov was White.

1.♖a7+ ♔f8! 2.♖d7! Averbakh's ! is correct. This rook move is the fastest route to victory. **2...♔g8**

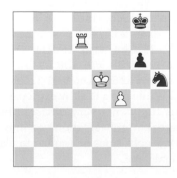

3.♔e6! Taimanov played 3.f5?, which must have been a great relief for Bronstein. After 3...gxf5 4.♔xf5 ♔f8! White will be unable to win. It's a fantastic idea not to swap the f-pawn, but to sacrifice it.

3...♘xf4+ 4.♔f6 ♘h5+ 5.♔xg6 ♘f4+ 6.♔g5 ♘e6+ 7.♔f6 ♘f4 8.♖d4 ♘e2 9.♖g4+ ♔f8 10.♖c4 ♔g8

11.♔g6

There's a quicker win here: 11.♔e5 is mate in 20. The black knight will be trapped after 11...♔f7 12.♖c7+ ♔f8 (or 12...♔g6 13.♖c2) 13.♖c2 ♘g3 14.♖h2, followed by 15.♔f4.

11...♔f8 12.♔g5 ♘g3 13.♔g4 ♘e2 14.♔f3 ♘g1+ 15.♔g2 ♘e2 16.♔f2 And White wins.

Systematic approach

In the 1950s, Averbakh formed a strong team of analysts to work on a four-volume endgame anthology: Vitaly Chekhover, Nikolai Kopayev, Viktor Khenkin and Ilya Maizelis. Together, they worked systematically on the various types of endgame. In 1956, the first part of the extensive series was published in Russian (in the 1980s a revised translation in five volumes appeared, *Comprehensive Chess Endings*). The part about bishop endings was written by Averbakh himself. It's striking how systematically he works through the various technical positions.

An example: last year, in Norway Chess, Magnus Carlsen won a bishop ending against Alireza Firouzja. The final phase doesn't really need any commentary.

Magnus Carlsen
Alireza Firouzja
Stavanger 2021 (6)

position after 46.♗xa6

White has just captured the a-pawn. The technical phase proceeds smoothly.

46...♗c6+ 47.♔d4 ♗e8 48.♗b7 ♗d7 49.♗f3 ♗c8 50.♗e2 ♗d7 51.♗d3 ♗c6 52.♗e4

Black resigned.

But how would it have gone if the black king had managed to reach square a6?

Averbakh had already answered this question 68 (!) years ago.

Yuri Averbakh
1954
White to play and win

1.♗f5 ♗f1 2.♔d4 ♗e2 3.♗d3! ♗g4 4.♔c5 ♗d7 5.♗f1 ♗e8 6.♗h3! Now Black is in zugzwang.

Averbakh had already answered this question 68 (!) years ago

Yuri Averbakh

1922	Born February 8th in Kaluga, 150 kilometres southwest of Moscow
1944	Awarded Master title
1949	Wins Moscow Championship
1952	International Grandmaster
1953	Zurich Candidates Tournament, shared 10th place
1954	Wins Soviet Championship ahead of Kortchnoi and Taimanov
1956	Shared first in Soviet Championship with Taimanov and Spassky, finishes 2nd in playoff
1956	FIDE International Judge of Chess Compositions
1958	Portoroz Interzonal, finishes shared 7th
1969	FIDE International Chess Arbiter
1973-78	Chairman Russian Chess Federation
1984	Chief arbiter first Karpov-Kasparov match in Moscow

A prolific journalist and author, Averbakh wrote many books on openings, endgames and chess history, and was the editor of the periodicals *Shahkmaty v SSSR*, *Shakhmatny Bulletin* and *Chess Herald* (in English and Russian).

In 2011 New In Chess published his memoir *Centre-Stage and Behind the Scenes*.

2022	Celebrates 100th birthday

6...♔b7 Or 6...♗f7 7.♗c8+, and the b-pawn will be lost. **7.♗g2+ ♔a6 8.♗c6** 1-0.

Douglas Griffin has this to say about Averbakh's endgame books in his blog: 'In the days of adjournments this series of books was an indispensable reference work for the tournament player.' Yet I usually took the books of the Swiss writer André Chéron – the other authority on theoretical endgames – with me to tournaments, mainly because he wrote

The top-finishers of the 1956 Soviet Championship: Mark Taimanov (who won the play-off), Yuri Averbakh and 19-year-old Boris Spassky.

more about rook endings – which are more numerous in practice.

It is interesting to compare Averbakh and Chéron. Chéron was a romantic who composed all kinds of complicated endgame studies – and problems. He could lose himself in page-long variations. Averbakh, on the other hand, concentrated on systematically researching basic positions in the endgame.

In many news items about his 100th birthday, he was also called 'a chess composer'. He wasn't, really. He does feature a lot in Van der Heijden's database, but his compositions are always about purely theoretical positions with just a few pieces, that are analysed to the very end.

Positive scores

Averbakh has a positive score against two World Champions: Max Euwe and Tigran Petrosian. He played Euwe just twice, in the 1953 Zurich Candidates tournament, winning both games. He beat Petrosian twice shortly after the war, both times as Black. His win in the 18th USSR Championship was very interesting. It's fascinating to see how radically

the perception of the opening and early middlegame has changed with the advent of the computer. Also striking is how Petrosian showed himself to be a fearless attacking player in his early years. It would take Petrosian nine years to have his revenge for this loss.

**Tigran Petrosian
Yuri Averbakh**
Moscow 1950
Queen's Gambit Declined, Moscow Variation

1.d4 d5 2.c4 e6 3.♘c3 c6 4.♘f3 dxc4 5.e4 b5 6.♗e2 ♗b7 7.0-0 ♘f6 8.a4 a6 9.♗g5 ♘bd7 10.e5 h6 11.♗h4 g5 12.♗g3 ♘d5

With transposition of moves, a position from the Moscow Variation has arisen. Averbakh does not comment on the

text. The knight was almost automatically played to the central square in those days. Nowadays, almost all top players would opt for 12...♘h5, a move that's also played if the knight is not attacked. This is because it is strategically justified to swap on g3, to deprive White of the bishop pair.

13.♘e4 Another standard knight move, although swapping on d5 would have been clearly stronger. This, too, is a case of growing insight. Petrosian probably not even considered swapping it, and Averbakh says nothing about it either. After 13.♘xd5 cxd5 14.♘e1! White has a dangerous plan, though: advancing the f-pawn and taking the king's bishop to h5, leaving a position that is just about tenable for Black. There could follow 14...bxa4 15.f4 ♕b6 16.♗h5 ♖h7 17.f5 0-0-0, and White is better, but Black needn't despair.

13...♕b6 14.♘d6+ ♗xd6 15.exd6 f6 A good strategic move to keep the white knight away from e5. Later, Averbakh indicated the advance 15...c5 as stronger, and it's true that this solves all Black's problems. White's best option is to aim for an endgame with 16.dxc5 ♕xc5 17.axb5 axb5 18.♖xa8+ ♗xa8 19.♕d4. After 19...0-0 20.♕xc5 ♘xc5 21.♘d4 White recaptures the pawn.

16.b4 An extremely interesting pawn sacrifice, but the computer sees it as a losing move.

The alternative 16.b3 is stronger, forcing Black to show his hand. 16...c3 is probably Black's best reaction, keeping the position as closed as possible. There could follow: 17.♘e1

0-0-0 18.♗f3 ♘b4 19.axb5 axb5 20.♘c2 ♘xc2 21.♕xc2 b4 22.♖fe1, and the position is dynamically balanced.

16...cxb3 Averbakh pays a lot of attention to 16...♘xb4 in his comments, but taking the second pawn is too dangerous. The main line goes as follows: 17.♕b1 ♘d5 18.♗g6+ ♔f8 19.♘e5 ♘xe5, and now 20.♗xe5! is far stronger than Averbakh's suggestion of 20.dxe5. After 20...♕d8 (20...fxe5 21.♗h5) 21.f4! ♕e8 22.♕e4! Black can't prevent the f-file from being opened.

So Averbakh was right to think better of accepting the second pawn offer. But is the text justified? He says: 'This exchange is forced, otherwise the bishop will be shut out of the game.' Again, the advent of the computer has deepened our insight, because Black can safely play 16...0-0-0. The bishop being cut off is of little consequence. The black structure is so solid that White has no starting-points for an initiative. There could follow 17.a5 ♕a7 18.♕d2 ♔b8 19.h4 ♔a8, and now the black queen can be redeployed via b8.

The text has two drawbacks: it allows the position to be opened, favouring White in view of his safer king, and it weakens Black's setup. The passed pawn on c4 deprives White of squares – e.g. d3 for the bishop – while possibly becoming an important trump in the endgame.

It also needs to be said that 16...0-0-0 does not definitively shut out the black bishop. It can be redeployed via c8 later.

17.♕xb3

17...♔f7
Black's best bet was probably going for counterplay with 17...h5. Play could get very sharp, with White probably claiming an edge. Here's a fascinating line: 18.♕c2 ♔f7 19.a5 ♕a7 20.♖ae1 ♖ag8 21.♕e4 ♗c8 22.♗d3 h4 23.♕xe6+ ♔g7 24.♕e4 ♘f8 25.♗e5 g4, and now 26.♖c1! is the correct move. All this is very complicated, and you could say that 17...h5 would have led to very unclear complications.

18.♖fe1 Obvious and natural, but 18.♕d1 was probably stronger. Withdrawing the queen is not such an obvious choice, but its purpose is clear: preventing the advance of the black h-pawn. 18...h5? 19.♘xg5+! fxg5 20.♗xh5+ ♔g7 21.♖e1 would give White a decisive attack.

18...♖ae8
Kind of a wasted move, really. Here, too, 18...h5 was the correct move to generate counterplay. There could follow: 19.h3 g4 20.a5 ♕a7, and now 21.♕d1! is again the correct move. If Black takes the knight, White will get a decisive attack; and if he doesn't, White will also be better.

19.♘e5+ 'Spectacular, but that is all', Averbakh observes drily, and he appears to be right.

The computer indicates 19.♕d1 as the strongest move, intending to meet 19...♚g7 with 20.♖c1, Remarkably enough, the computer regards this position as winning for White, not least because there are no concrete threats. A closer look reveals that Black is in deep trouble. His king is permanently exposed, and he has no chance to create counterplay. In addition, the white d6-pawn is strong, allowing White to reinforce his position at leisure.

19...♘xe5

Certainly not 19...fxe5 20.♗h5+ ♚f8 21.dxe5, and White reigns supreme.

20.dxe5 f5 21.♗h5+ ♚g7 22.a5

Closing the a-file was unnecessary. White's best bet would have been 22.♗xe8 ♖xe8 23.h4, e.g. 23...c5 24.axb5 axb5 25.♖eb1 ♗c6, and the position is equal.

22...♕a7 23.♗xe8 ♖xe8 24.h4 c5

25.hxg5

A serious error. Opening the h-file only helps Black.

25...hxg5 26.♕d1 ♖h8 27.f3 c4+

Too hasty. Black needn't have acted on the queenside yet. With 27...♚g6 he could have decisively reinforced his position. The king is excellently placed on g6, and Black has a dangerous plan: moving the bishop and directing the queen to h7, putting the white king into serious trouble.

28.♗f2 ♕b8 29.♕d4 ♕e8 30.♕a7 ♕c6 31.♕c5

31...c3

'Typical time-trouble play, in which the main thing is not to blunder anything away', Averbakh observes. Yet the pawn move is a weakening, because Black's structure wasn't solid enough yet to support the c-pawn. 31...♚g6! would have been strong again here, intending to meet 32.♖ad1 with 32...♕d7. The queen

52.♖h1 The black pawns are unstoppable. After 52.♗d4, 52...♘c3 would have decided the issue.
52...c1♕ 53.♖axc1 ♖xc1 54.♖xc1 b2 55.♖h1 ♘c3 56.♗c5 b1♕ 57.♖xb1 ♘xb1 58.♗b4

White has still managed to shut in the black knight, but Black eventually manages to free it.
58...♚e8 59.♚e3 ♚d7 60.♚d4 ♚c6 61.♚c4 ♗d1 62.♚d3 ♗b3 63.♚d4 ♗c2 64.♚c4 ♗a4 65.♚d4 ♗b5

Zugzwang. White is forced to let the black knight go, and now things will go downhill fast.
66.♗e1 ♘a3 67.♗d2 ♗f1 68.♗c1 ♘c4
White resigned. ■

The Chess Museum on Gogolevsky Boulevard in the heart of Moscow can be seen as one of the many achievements of Yuri Averbakh (here together with curator Tatyana Kolesnikovich in 2014).

---

can now go to h7, and White would be virtually on the ropes.

32.♖ec1
Petrosian aims for the queenside, but 32.♖ad1! would have been far stronger. In many cases, White can now return the exchange by taking on d5, with equality. An illustrative variation: 32...♖c8 33.♕xc6 ♗xc6 34.♗b6 b4 35.♖xd5 ♗xd5 36.d7 ♖a8 37.d8♕ ♖xd8 38.♗xd8 b3 39.♗b6 b2 40.♗d4, with a drawn opposite-coloured bishops endgame.
32...♕d7 33.♖ab1 ♖c8
For the third time, 33...♚g6 would have been strong. Taking the queen to h7 remains a dangerous plan for White.

34.♕a7
White should have withdrawn his queen with 34.♕d4. After 34...♖c4 35.♕d3 ♘f4 36.♕f1 g4 37.♗e3 he has good chances of a successful defence.
34...♖c4 35.♕b8 ♖c8 36.♕a7 ♖c4 37.♕b8 ♕c8 38.♕a7 ♕c6 39.♕b8 ♕d7 40.♕a7 ♚g6

Finally. Just before the time-control, Averbakh hits on the correct plan.
41.♗e1 b4 42.♖b3
The sealed move. White has nothing to hope for; Black's passed pawns are too strong.
42...♗c8 43.♕a8 ♕c6 44.♕xc6 ♖xc6 45.g3 ♗d7 46.♗f2 g4 47.f4 ♖c8 48.♗b6 ♚f7 49.♖bb1 ♗a4 50.♚f2 c2 51.♖a1 b3

Jonas Buhl Bjerre

CURRENT ELO: 2601

DATE OF BIRTH: June 26, 2004

PLACE OF BIRTH: Silkeborg, Denmark

PLACE OF RESIDENCE: Bjedstrup, Denmark

What is your favourite city?
Copenhagen.

What was the last great meal you had?
During the Copenhagen light festival, with my girlfriend in a small Asian restaurant!

What drink brings a smile to your face?
All drinks with an exotic name, and an unreasonable amount of fruit in it.

Which book would you give to a friend?
I enjoyed Philip Kerr's novels about Bernie Gunther a lot.

Which book are you currently reading?
Muhammad Ali, His Life and Times by Thomas Hauser. Highly recommended!

What is your all-time favourite movie?
I feel terribly unqualified to answer this question, as I have not watched the classics. Recently I enjoyed *Don't look up*.

And your favourite TV series?
How I Met Your Mother.

Do you have a favourite actor?
Neil Patrick Harris.

And a favourite actress?
Chelsea Peretti.

What is your earliest chess memory?
My first European Youth Championship in Prague 2012. I lost the first two rounds, but had an amazing time the entire event anyway.

Who is your favourite chess player?
Garry Kasparov. An outstanding player and fighter, and the founder of the Kasparov Chess Foundation, which has helped me immensely over the last couple of years by providing me with many hours of high-class coaching.

Is there a chess book that had a profound influence on you?
The first books that got me hooked on chess were the *Steps* tactics books. I would solve them in the early hours, when I was unable to sleep.

What was your best result ever?
Winning the gold medal on Board 3 at the European Teams 2021 with a performance rating of 2793.

And the best game you played?
Bjerre-Adhiban, 2021 Grand Swiss.

What was the most exciting chess game you ever saw?
Bjerre-Ganguly, which can be seen with my comments in this very issue!

What is your favourite square?
d5.

Do chess players have typical shortcomings?
They tend to see everything in black and white.

Facebook, Instagram, Snapchat, or?
I am not a big user of social media. Actually Facebook and Snapchat are the only ones I have.

How many friends do you have on Facebook?
438.

When was the last time you cried?
During my latest attempt to break down the Berlin Defence.

What is your life motto?
Mañana, mañana. Not purposely though.

Who or what would you like to be if you weren't yourself?
My childhood dream was to become a professional soccer player.

Which three people would you like to invite for dinner?
Cristiano Ronaldo, Dwayne Johnson, Muhammad Ali.

Is there something you'd love to learn?
How to drive a car, how to run a marathon, how to beat my girlfriend at draughts.

What would people be surprised to know about you?
I am unsurprisingly surprisingly unsurprising. I also eat more slowly than a turtle.

What is your greatest fear?
I find birds rather intimidating.

If you could change one thing in the chess world, what would it be?
Have more women play chess.

What does it mean to be a chess player?
A lot of hard work, many ups and downs, a lot of travelling, and a lot of great experiences with great people.

Is a knowledge of chess useful in everyday life?
I don't think so, but I do think that it's very rewarding.

What is the best thing that was ever said about chess?
'Those who say they understand chess understand nothing.' – Robert Hübner.